A Synthesis of Alchemy

An Inquiry into the Secrets of Hermetic Philosophy

Dorje Jinpa

Pentarba Publications

Also by Dorje Jinpa

SENSA: The Language of the Sacred Mysteries

Essential Teachings of Maitreya: Three Complete Works

Secrets of the Heart: Awakening to Enlightenment

The Book of Hermes

The Coming Avatar: An Essay on the Reappearance of the Christ

Knights of the Sacred Fire: An Introduction to the Agni Yoga Teachings

Gates to Infinity: A Commentary on the Agni Yoga Infinity Teachings

Available at pentarba.com

First edition hardback 1994 (100 copies)
Second revised and enlarged edition hardback 2016 (100 copies)
2018 (100 copies) hardback
2023 (100 copies) hardback

Sold online at pentarba.com

Contents

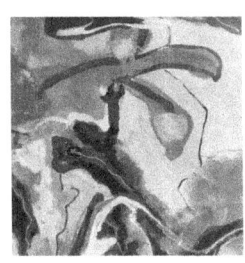

Vulcan's hammer strikes
And radiant sparks of celestial Light
Descend into the darkness,
Where they are gathered together
And condensed into a single point of radiance.

The eye of Horus thus becomes the Blazing Star
That guides the pilgrim's steps
Through the triple caves of darkness.

The Tears of Isis descend
Drop by drop into the holy Chalice,
Where they are condensed into Soma,
The elixir of the Gods,
And crystallized into the wondrous Pearl of Sophia.

The white seed of the sun unites with the red egg of the moon,
And in the fire of their union is conceived
The golden embryo of the Child of the Sun.

With reverence we bow
to the Great White Brotherhood
Who guide and protect
the spiritual Evolution of the world.

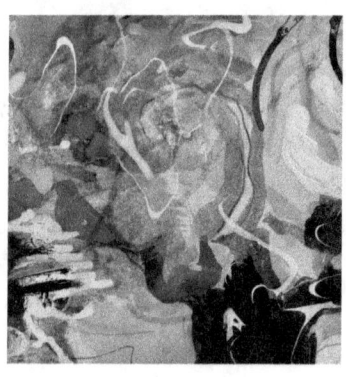

Introduction

The Great Work is both in us and about us.

Hermes Trismegistus

The transmutation of one element into another has for over 350 years been considered impossible. And while scientists have now successfully demonstrated transmutation in the laboratory, most people still classify alchemy with superstition and wishful thinking. In 1919 Nobel Prize Laureate Ernest Rutherford discovered that while transmutation seemed to be impossible through mere chemical means (i.e. the exchange of electrons of the peripheral shell of the atom) it could be produced in nitrogen and oxygen by exposing the nuclei of their atoms to radioactive particles of a suitable type.[1] By 1937 practically all known elements were found to be capable of transmutation on a small scale. Even minute quantities of gold were produced from a variety of other elements including lead, though the cost of the procedure far outweighed any profits from the venture.[2] In 1959 biologist Louis Kervran successfully demonstrated that the transmutation of one element into another occurs naturally in nature.[3] This confirmed statements made by many practicing alchemists, including Baron von Herzeele[4] and Rudolf Steiner.[5] And while

---

[1] Ernest Rutherford. *The Transmutation of Matter.* The Royal Institution 1930

[2] Ernest Rutherford. *The Transmutation of Heavy Elements.* The Royal Institution, 1937.

[3] Louis Kervran. *Biological Transmutation.* Brooklyn, 1972.

[4] Von Herzeele published over 500 experiments between 1876 and 1883 indicating the transmutation of the elements within organic substance. Rudolf Hauschka Hailmittellehre. Frankfort 1965, chapter IX.

scientists do yet understand how this spontaneous transmutation works, the fact remains; it does exist and it can no longer be denied. But of course the bias of centuries is difficult to overcome.

In ancient times science and the religious mystery was viewed as one and the same subject. This approach to the mysteries of life has been forgotten. Scientists and theologians have nothing to say to each other. The truth of the ancient sages that "Matter is a dense form of spirit and spirit is a subtle state of matter," has been forgotten. The stark division between the physical and spiritual, between religion and science, is one of the primary causes for misunderstanding the ancient esoteric writings.

Modern students of the Hermetic Mysteries have for some time debated whether alchemy, as practiced by the ancient initiates, was a physical or a spiritual practice. Manly P. Hall, the great esoteric historian, has stated that the methodology of physical alchemy was a blind, an allegorical veil, for instructions in spiritual alchemy, the transformation of ordinary consciousness into the undivided spiritual consciousness. And while this is indeed true, the reverse is also true; that in the process of soul transformation lies hidden the secrets of physical transmutation. 'As above, so below.' The few alchemists who understood this veiled in their writings by presenting spiritual truths using chemical terminology and chemical truths using theological references. Without the master key of synthesis and correspondence the ancient alchemical writings are difficult to decipher. The true secret of alchemy, however, lies not with one or the other, but with both, physical and spiritual, together as one natural process the goal of which is the spiritualization of matter and the human consciousness.

The fundamental principles of alchemy and the Hermetic sciences can be directly traced to the Ancient Mysteries. Primary among these principles is the Law of Correspondence as given in the Emerald Tablet of Hermes. "True and without error, certain and most true; that which is above is like that which is below, and that which is below is like that which is above." Due to the oneness and interdependence of the universe the laws of nature, when understood, can be accurately applied in kind to all

---

5 Rudolf Steiner. *Agriculture*, London 1974, from lectures given in 1924.

levels of the multidimensional universe.[1] "Since psychic energy is an energy," writes Master M, "it will not contradict the laws of physics."[2]

The secret fire of the alchemists, the Azoth and *primum ens* of Paracelsus, the Vital Light of Hermes Trismegistus, is psychic energy, the divine spark of livingness within all living organisms. This is not physical fire or even etheric energy, though it will manifests itself through the etheric body, the essence and prototype of the physical body. It is this radiant energy that give power to thought creativeness and is used by initiates to produce transmutation on all levels of the Work. It should not be forgotten that all atoms, even atoms of the mineral kingdom were considered by the Hermetic philosophers to be living organisms. Isaac Newton wrote several books on the aliveness of matter, none of which have ever been published.

"To produce the transmutation of any substance," writes Paracelsus, "we must first draw the Azoth to a central point" within the organism. Thus by drawing the fire of the philosophers to a point of focus the volatile essence is stimulated and thus transmutation ensues. When working with the human organism there are of course several points of vital essence, sometimes called 'points of tension,' that might be considered.

One of the primary principles upon which the 'Great Work' is based is the essential unity of all things; that in essence all things, animate and inanimate, have a common basis and origin. When applied to the material sphere this common essential nature is called the *prima materia*, or first matter. The ancient Greeks called this primary energy-substance 'aether.' In modern occultism, as presented through Theosophy and the works of Alice Bailey and Rudolf Steiner, this vital essence is generally referred to as etheric matter. If physical substance could be reduced to its primary condition, its *prima materia*, the alchemists reasoned, it could then be built upon in such a way as to produce any known element or substance.

---

[1] See Chapter 1 of my *SENSA: The Sacred Language of the Ancient Mysteries.*

[2] AUM 537

"Metals can be transmuted one into another," writes Thomas Aquinas, "since they are of one and same original matter."[1]

The truth of essential unity can be applied equally well to the macrocosm or metaphysical universe. When applied to the evolution of consciousness, for example, we see that the original *prima* condition pertains to the spiritual consciousness, or what the Buddhists call Bodhi, primordial awareness. At this level the alchemical process is applied to the transformation of the consciousness back to its original primordial condition, 'the mind in the natural state,' as the great Buddhist yogi Naropa expressed it. According to the Vajrayana scriptures on the subject, once this state has been attained the vajra (etheric) body[2] is spontaneously transformed into a wondrous rainbow body of light. The original Mind, (*Alayavijnana*), is to the individual consciousness what the *prima materia* or etheric matter, is to the physical world. In other words there is a working analogy, between the two, not in the details but in principle.

Only by approaching the subject of alchemy holistically as a synthesis can we gain an understanding of the principles involved. The Law of Synthesis affirms that there is no boundary line, no hard and fast distinction, between spirit and matter. Paracelsus maintained that it was the unity of the spiritual and the corporeal worlds that made transmutation possible. Albert Einstein expressed the truth of synthesis in terms of physics. "There is no essential distinction," he said, "between mass [matter] and energy."[7] The theory of relativity has produced new definitions of matter and energy. Matter is now defined as energy whose vibrational activity is slower than the speed of light, while energy is defined as matter whose vibrational activity is greater than the speed of light.[3] The only difference, therefore, between matter and energy is the relative speed of their particles. Scientists are slowly moving toward agreement with much that was taught by the adepts of ageless Mystery Tradition who say that 'all

---

[1] Translated by Mary Atwood, and quoted in her *A Suggestive Inquiry into Hermetic Mystery*, page 33.

[2] Vajra is a Sanskrit term used in Buddhist Tantric scriptures to the mean indestructible essential nature. The 'vajra body' is the etheric body, the essence and archetype of the dense physical body.

[7] Albert Einstein and Leopold Infeld. *The Evolution of Physics*. N.Y. 1951, p. 208.

[3] Perhaps it will be discovered that thought is energy vibrating faster than the speed of light.

is energy,' one all pervading Cosmic Fire, from the dense crystalized energy of matter to the subtle, high vibrational activity of consciousness and spirit. Matter, say the illuminated Sages, contains the consciousness principle, and consciousness is a subtle energy. Thus the division of the world into animate and inanimate, mind and form, spiritual and physical, is an illusion, for like energy and matter, there is no essential distinction between the two.

There is an ancient prophecy that points to the present time, which states that the secret Temple, whose doors have remained closed except for those few who could prove their worthiness, will now open its doors to all who wish to enter. This prophecy pertains to the restoration of the ancient Mystery Schools of initiation. It is the purpose of this book to aid in the restoration of the Mysteries.

Some Fundamental Principles

As [the energies] descend they produce stimulation; as they ascend they produce transmutation and abstraction. Djwhal Khul

The Yogis hold that matter (in itself) does not exist, but is a form of energy, which energy is a form of mind, which mind is manifestation of the Absolute. Ramacharaka

Mind is the father and cause of bodies and souls, both of which subsist and are energized by the mind. Proclus

Alchemy is a spiritual science, which through the application of fire (energy) quickens the natural processes of evolution in any of the kingdoms of nature to a point where the indwelling life, its volatile essence, naturally discards its old form, to take upon itself, naturally or under the alchemist's direction, a new form more in harmony with its now quickened vibration and in line with its natural evolutionary direction and purpose.

Solomon Trismosin, the reputed teacher of Paracelsus, noted at the beginning of his *Splendor Solis*, that the Philosopher's Stone is produced by means of 'green and growing nature,' in other words, through the natural process of evolution itself. The alchemist does not initiate anything artificial or unnatural. Patanjali beautifully expresses this idea in his *Yoga Sutras* (IV 2 & 3):

> *Transmutation occurs naturally as a result of the innate creative forces of nature and not through the methods and practices, which but clear away the obstacles, as the farmer clears the field for sowing.*

The alchemist creates those conditions that make the subject ripe for transmutation. Nature does the rest.

According to the Adepts there is life in all things or, as Plato states it, 'all things are full of gods.' Isaac Newton wrote extensively on hylozoism, the theory that matter is alive, yet because of the bias of scientists his writings on the subject have never been published. Isaac Newton left behind an extensive library of manuscripts, in his own hand, on Hermetic and Pythagorean science, alchemy, and hylozoism. This great lifetime achievement was inspected after his death by prominent members of the Royal Society and marked 'not for publication.' To this day, except for minor fragments, these writings have not been published, even as historical curiosities! Newton agreed with the Pythagoreans that the sun, stars, and planetary bodies, including the Earth, are alive—that they are animate rather than inanimate bodies. "All matter is living matter," says Brother D.K.[1]

In the Hermetic Mysteries it is taught that the inner activity of Nature is made up of numerable invisible lives, from the tiny elemental entities that are the sum total of all physical-etheric forms, through the nature spirits, lesser and greater, that nourish and maintain the organic life-forms of nature, the great Devas that oversee the working of nature on all levels, to the Great Goddess of Nature Herself. Working with these fiery lives without the development of self-mastery and without the necessary knowledge is dangerous. The old adage concerning playing with fire is

---

[1] Alice Bailey *A Treatise on Cosmic Fire*, page 488.

appropriate. As one Adept stated it, "Nothing is more dangerous than too much energy."

Chung Pu-taun, the Taoist alchemist, once wrote:

What you see is not used. What is used is not seen.

The chemist works with the dense physical aspects of matter, the peripheral shell of the atoms, while the alchemist works with its etheric nature through the application of the alchemical fire (psychic-energy). The alchemist works with causes, which have a direct effect upon the dense physical plane. The chemist works only with the world of effects.

The profound works attributed to Hermes, especially his *Golden Treatise, The Emerald Tablet,* and *The Divine Pymander* can be counted among the greatest of western alchemical texts. As in the esoteric literature of the East, the short highly veiled affirmations contained in these texts are condensed and simplified explanations of very complex processes of cosmic as well as individual and even physical significance. To the illuminated mind each sentence contains a wealth of information. In the *Emerald Tablet* we read:

It ascends from earth to heaven,
And again descends to the earth,
Receiving thereby the virtues of both.

This statement pertains to the law of cycles, an important aspect of evolutionary process on all levels. The descent of spirit into form and diversity—involution and the ascent of spirit back to the unity of the higher worlds evolution—evolution, to be repeated ad-infinitum. To this is added qualities and knowledge developed and refined through the process. In the old alchemical texts descent and ascent respectively apply to densification and spiritualization. By applying the Hermetic Law, 'As above, so below,' we see that the law of cycles applies in all areas of the evolutionary process including those as perceived in the fundamental laws of natures, and the evolution of consciousness.

Its application to alchemy is to be found in the verse that precedes it.

Thou shalt separate the fire from the earth,
The subtle from the dense,
Gently and with much attention.
It ascends from earth to heaven
And again descends to the earth,
Receiving, thereby, the virtues of each.

The alchemists, no matter on what level she wishes to apply her art, always works with energy, subtle energy, and very subtle psychic energy. Let us not forget that, as modern science has demonstrated, the atom is crystalized energy. But what science has yet to discover is that like the human being as a whole, atoms contain a hidden spiritual essence. The alchemist is instructed to first abstract out the vital essence (*spiritus vita*), from the outer substance, 'gently with much attention', in other words, without losing it. The exodus, or what Hermes called 'the liberation of the Heavenly Flyer,' 'the wine of the philosophers' (mercury), liberates the fiery essence from its imprisonment in form. This destroys the enclosing outer and inner form. The subtle energy must ascends from earth to heaven, from the dense physical plane to the etheric, the *prima materia*, before it can be clothed with its new prototype. To extract the essence from the matter, to be clothed in a new form, it must first be hermetically sealed in a subtle crucible, a 'ring pass not.' Otherwise it will fly back to its source. According to Mary Atwood in her alchemical masterpiece *A Suggestive Inquiry into the Hermetic Mystery*[1] the 'crucible,' and what exactly it contains, is one of the primary mysteries of alchemy.

When transmutation takes place in the cosmos it is called *Pralaya*, the death and rebirth of the objective universe. For a human being it is called initiation, the liberation (*moksha*) of the soul from its imprisonment in form, leading to its regenerated descent again as an initiate involved in the Great or One Work of Evolution.

---

[1] Page

In plant alchemy (spagyrics), as taught by Paracelsus, John Heydon and others, the volatile essence of a medicinal herb is first extracted as a tincture and then extracted again through distillation. The 'Heavenly Flyer' is thus retained in the distillate and can be latter administered to the patient as a powerful elixir. This is what Homeopathy attempts to achieve. The ascent of the qualified subtle essence is accomplished through the application of psychic energy (*azoth*). John Heydon gives this subtle hint:

> *And by this means you have a most subtle essence, which being held over a gentle heat will fly up into the glass and represent the perfect idea of that vegetable whereof it is the essence.*[1]

The key word here is 'idea.' It is the 'subtle essence,' which contains the 'perfect idea of the vegetable,' its medicinal nature, that is extracted from the matter, to become thereby a powerful healing elixir.

Basil Valentine, one of the greatest of the 15th-cntury alchemists, says that digestion and putrefaction are the master keys to the process.[2] Through heat and the digestive fluids of the body, the nutritive elements of food are transmuted into a subtle energy that is then absorbed in the blood, which via the bloodstream regenerates the physical cells of the body, leaving behind the old form to disintegrate (putrefy) as waste. It should be remembered, however, that there is a big difference in alchemy between the destruction of the form through the liberation of its central essence and the liberation of the essence through the destruction of the form. The former conforms to natural law; the latter, does not. To merely destroy the outer form, as some alchemists seem to advocate, does not liberate the central essence so that it can be re-clothed in a new form. The same is true for the liberation/transformation of a human being. To destroy the body will not liberate the soul. The transmutation and regeneration of the physical-etheric body is brought about as the result of a spiritual impulse, a stimulation of the spiritual fire or energy descending from above. To

---

[1] *The Holy Guide*, page 54. On page 74 there is this heading: 'To make the idea of any plant appear in the glass as if the very plant itself were there,.'
[2] *The Triumphal Chariot of Antimony.*

attempt to transmute and rejuvenate the physical-etheric body without this spiritual impulse is impossible beyond a certain point, for while the body can be vitalized to some degree without this spiritual impulse, complete transmutation and regeneration will only occur through the integration, the alchemical wedding, with the higher vehicles. The same is generally true with physical and biological alchemy.

In the following pages three basic fields of application will be considered, physical, spiritual, and secret.

1. The transmutation of etheric matter, and by reflex physical substance, from one state to another *finer* state. This includes both organic and inorganic substances.

2. The transformation and abstraction of the consciousness principle from the limitations of the form world (physical, emotional, and mental) into the higher states of clear spiritual perception and being.

3. The natural culmination of these two processes as they come to fruition in the human kingdom. Its goal is the transformation of consciousness *plus* its three vehicles of expression, mental, emotional, and etheric, into the *trikaya*, the three regenerated bodies or vehicles of a fully realized Arhat or Adept. It deals with the transfiguration of the life-conscious-continuum from the fourth kingdom, the purely human, to the fifth kingdom of nature.

When applied to the physical-etheric plane the process is called transmutation. When applied to the human consciousness it is called transformation. When the process becomes complete in the human kingdom it is called transfiguration.

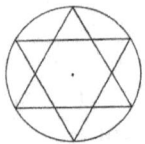

The Symbolic Language of the Mysteries

The symbolism of the Ancient Wisdom is based on the comparison of the macrocosm with the microcosm.

Agni Yoga

All alchemical symbols, phrases, and metaphors, which so disguise the art, are more than what they seem. They point out a reality and were we in the spirit of their truth we should find them to be far more literally true than they are thought to be.

Mary Atwood

H ermetic science is a direct expression of the Ancient Mysteries. As such its teachings have always been deeply veiled in symbols. The purpose of this was to keep the teachings pure and free from distortions and to prevent the harm that is sure to arise from revealing too much to those who are not yet ready to make use of the information in a responsible manner. The Adepts of the Mystery Tradition understood that only those students of high moral character, the essential prerequisite of an awakened spiritual intuition, a facility higher than the rational mind, could safely receive the teachings. The Teaching of the Mysteries, which were considered to be revelations of the Gods, were considered to be too sacred to be given to the masses. Thus they were veiled in such a way that only those who were advanced spiritually would be able to understand the hidden meaning.

One of the ways in which authentic alchemical texts were veiled was by substituting a physical principle or substance for its intended higher ethereal or spiritual counterpart. When the alchemist Roger Bacon said, "Though I say take this or that, believe me not, but operate according to the blood," he means to use the corresponding vital essence, symbolized by the blood. Thus 'gold' is often a blind for 'philosopher's gold,' the vital essence of gold, its etheric archetype. Poetic phrases like 'dragon's blood' or 'the blood of the lion' refer to the essential nature, the volatile essence, of matter, the universal tincture from which all things physical arise. Another example of this is that when the word fire or light is used in the ancient texts it can simply be read as energy. When Paracelsus, for example, speaks of the multiplicity of fire, he is speaking of the many degrees of subtle energy, which he says corresponds to the fire/energy of the planets.[1] When we are told to invoke the Light from above this should be taken literally, as real spiritual energy.

"The key that is to open one," says Homer, "must open all, otherwise it cannot be the right key." The master key to the Hermetic Mysteries, as well to the laws of nature, which they depict, is the Law of Analogy or Correspondence as given in the *Emerald Tablet* of Hermes, 'as it is above, so it is below.' The archetypal symbols used are never arbitrarily chosen, but rather depict geometric or natural images that actually correspond, on higher and lower levels, with a fundamental truth or principle.

Paracelsus gives this veiled, yet valuable hint, concerning the Law of Correspondence:

> If I have 'manna' in my constitution, I can attract 'manna form heaven.'
> Melissa [lemon balm] is not only in my garden, but also in the air and in

<hr>

[1] *The Archidoxes of Magic*

heaven. Saturn is not only in the sky, but also deep in the earth and in the ocean. What is Venus but Artemisia [Mugwort] that grows in your garden? What is iron but mars? That is to say, Venus and Artemisia are both the products of the same essence, and mars and iron are both the manifestation of the same root cause. What is the human body but a constellation of the same powers that are contained in the stars in the sky? He who knows iron knows the attributes of Mars. He who knows Mars knows the qualities of iron. What would become of your heart if there were no sun in the universe? What would be the use of your 'vasa spermatica' [creative energies] if there were no Venus? To grasp the invisible [etheric] elements, to attract them by their material correspondences, to control, purify, and transform them by the living power of spirit [Vulcan]—this is true alchemy.[1]

Another example of this law can be found in the mythological Mt. Meru, a symbol used in the esoteric literature of both Hindus and Buddhists to secretly represent the central magnetic axis of the earth. By applying the Law of Analogy this archetypal symbol represents the *axis mundi* for all life forms, whether an atom of matter, a human being, a planet, or a solar system (*Sumeru*). Mt. Meru is to the earth what the *sutratma*, the etheric spinal column, is to the human body. In the *Book of Light* (*Sefer ha-Zohar*) this idea is symbolized by the Tree of Life, whose roots (where it takes nourishment) are in the heavens and its braches and fruit (the etheric nerve centers) are below (in manifestation). This idea is rather acurately symbolized in the Staff of Hermes:

The wings may represent the radiant whirl of the two petaled ajna center as can be clairvoyantly observed extending out from the two sides of the head of very creative individuals.

---

[1] Paragranum

Most of the symbols used in veiling the esoteric teaching are either natural or geometric. Master D.K. gives a few basic examples.[1]

1. The cross in its varying forms.
2. The lotus.
3. The triangle.
4. The cube.
5. The sphere and the point.
6. Eight animal forms, the goat, the bull, the elephant, the man, the dragon, the bear, the lion, and the dog.
7. The line.
8. Certain signs of the Zodiac.
9. The cup or Holy Grail.

Some occult books combine both natural and geometric symbols. Natural symbols often hint at a meaning through similarity of purpose and use. The Golden Fleece, for example, is a natural symbol meaning golden or radiant skin, the magnetic etheric body on one level and the perfected Luminous Body on another. Sometimes the shape of a natural symbol will be used to suggest a geometrical one. The Holy Grail is such a symbol, although its natural use gives us a hint as to its geometric meaning.

In the same way that sand forms geometric patterns in response to certain sounds, so when psychic energy, the energy and creative power of thought, is directed and qualified with purpose it produces in the ethers a glyph of geometric proportions. When the subtle vibrations of creative thought align themselves with fundamental principles the glyphs take on symmetrical form. This is the origin of many ancient esoteric symbols. Geometrical symbols are thus stylized depictions in line, shape, number, color, and tone, of the archetypal energy patterns of fundamental principles in nature. They depict, often presented in a stylized form, the lines of force

---

[1] *Initiation Human and Solar* (pages 165 & 166) by Alice Bailey.

inherent in the conceptual activity of those principles. According to Plato and latter Proclus, the esoteric commentator of Plato's works, the Idea-forms (*eidos*), the archetypal blueprints behind all manifested life in nature, can be accurately represented by geometrical forms.

The Pythagoreans taught that numbers are a direct expression of fundamental principles and therefore represent causes rather then effects.[1] In one sense, numbers represent the evolutionary sequence and stages by which fundamental principles manifest into form—the One into many and the many back to the One.

The colour of these symbols, representations of fundamental conceptual forms, represents quality. The lines represent lines of force, directions of the flow of energy. As the material plane as a whole is represented by the "four square" (double duality—vertical and horizontal) we can divide most geometric symbols into four directions—North (up), South (down), East (right), and West (left). North and South together represent the vertical spirit-matter axes, energy-form, noumena-phenomena, involution-evolution, in and out, etc. The horizontal axis represents the pairs of opposites active on the same plane—male and female, positive and negative, creative and receptive etc. If we take the equal armed cross $+$ to represent the evolution of the human spirit we see that the vertical axes, the path of ascent, is attained by progressively balancing the pairs of opposites on the horizontal plane. In this we have the mathematical formula for the evolution of consciousness. If we add to this formula the symbols of the illuminated mind present within threefold spiritual Being we have the glyph of an initiate alchemist of a certain degree active the Great Work of human salvage. Fundamental hieroglyphs have their own corresponding vibrational frequencies or sound equivalent.

To the Magi of ancient Persians those glyphs that accurately represent principles and laws of Nature were called Sensa, Language of the Sun.[2] The adepts of the ancient Mysteries are said to have used this

---

[1] One of the best writings on the esoteric meaning of numbers can be found in *The Key to the Universe* and *The Key to Destin* written by an anonymous Elder Brother and published under the name of his student Harriette Curtiss.

[2] See my book, *SENSA Language of the Sun.*

language to communicate in secret with each other as well the higher Masters of the Brotherhood. According to the most ancient esoteric tradition, which can be occultly traced through both the East and West, it is a form of this language that is used by gods to direct the creative forces of nature. It is for this reason, we are told, that the creative power the Sensa alphabet has always been kept secret from the uninitiated. According to Master D.K. aspects of this most sacred language are progressively revealed at each initiation into the Mysteries.

The above hieroglyph (from hiero meaning sun and glyph meaning sign) demonstrates the hidden relationship between the numbers one, three, seven, and ten united on three levels—the one spirit manifesting as the three fold consciousness principle on the seven planes or levels of energy/substance. This idea is also represented by the Tetractys of Pythagoras, which is said to be the master key to his philosophy. The three fundamental principles (spirit, consciousness, and primary energy-form) encompasses the seven evolutionary qualities indicating the future ten fold completion of the manifestation.

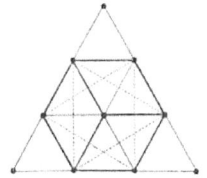

"The seven," says the *Sefer Yetzirah*, "can be depicted as three opposite three, with the one to rule and to decide between them."[1]

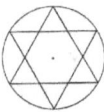

One of the ways in which the language of the Mysteries has been used, especially in alchemical literature, is to represent a principle in nature with the symbol of its corresponding metal or with its archetype, one of the planetary Gods. The Hermetic philosophers Paracelsus and Van Welling used this system of correspondence freely. In this connection it should be noted that Mercury is the name for both the planet and its corresponding metal, with the added meaning for astrologers, of intelligence. In Sanskrit the planet Mercury is called *Buddhi* with exactly the same three levels of meaning—the planet, the mineral, and intelligence—although in both cases it is spiritual intelligence that is meant and not the rational mind, which is a but a modern materialistic distortion.

In most alchemical literature the three fundamental principles when applied to the physical/etheric plane was represented by:

1) Mercury, the spirit of matter,
2) Sulphur, the soul-fire of matter, and
3) and Salt, it's crystalized material form.

Mercury is geometrically depicted by the glyph ☿. This represents the central fire or volatile essence of matter, symbolized by the sun ☉ united with the passive receptive energies of matter symbolized by the moon ☾, manifesting ↓ into form ✝. Sulphur, which is geometrically depicted by the glyph ♁, represents the soul-fire or quality of matter, the consciousness principle △ manifesting ↓ in form ✝. Salt, as depicted by the glyph ⊖, represents the vital electrical quality of etheric matter, which

---

[1] 6:5

manifests through the interaction of the primary pairs of opposites at the two horizontal poles. This symbol is also appropriately used to represent ecology.

The alchemical trinity—mercury, sulphur, and salt—is also used to represent three alchemical processes. Salt is a symbol for the crystallization-materialization process, the fixing of the volatile, a process that will eventually produce Soma and the Philosopher's Stone.

Sulphur (soul fire) works under the Law of Attraction drawing down the spiritual fire, which through an intensification of its essential nature, acts as an ascending transmuting agent. Jacob Boehme, in his *Three Principles of Divine Essence*, gives some of the seed-syllables contained in the term SULPHUR according to the Sacred Language:

> *The syllable SUL signifies and is the Soul of a Thing, for in the Word it is Light [UR] that is generated out of the syllable PHUR...[FIRE] The syllable PHUR is the Prima Materia [first matter] and contains in itself the third Principle.*[1]

Mercury, which is often used as a symbol for the volatile essence of matter, represents, on a higher turn of the spiral, the central spark of livingness within all Nature, within all living organisms. "Mercury," writes Fulcanelli in his alchemical masterpiece, *The Mystery of the Cathedrals*, "is the bird of Hermes." In the *Golden Treatise* of Hermes it is called the 'Heavenly Flyer,' for like the Phoenix, it rises from the ashes of the old form to become reborn in a radiant new form. Alchemy therefore might well be called magic for regardless of what level the alchemist is working to materialize the new form, elemental entities are involved. This can take place either naturally, in step with evolution, or not. When in harmony with ecological path we have white magic or dharma, when out of step we have karma.

Paracelsus, in the opening paragraph of his *Treatise on the Threefold Essence*, writes:

---

[1] Jacob Behman, *The Three Principles of Divine Essence*, Yoga Publications, page 20

Everything that is generated and produced of its elements is divided into three, namely, into Salt, Sulphur, and Mercury. Out of these a conjunction takes place — one body and a united essence. This does not concern the body in its outward aspect, but only the internal nature of the body.[1]

The 'internal nature of the body,' its true nature, is the etheric or energy body. It contains the three Principles. The physical body is considered to be a maya, an illusive reflection of its internal nature, and is therefore not considered by initiates to be a principle.

Essentially the three are one, but outwardly in the physical world they are seemingly separate. The greater the integration or union between these three principles the closer that organism is to perfection and thereby to its transmutation to the next level of being. When the three fires of the etheric body of any living entity (the alchemists considered matter to be alive) are fully united they produce the exodus of the Mercury, the Heavenly Flyer, which if not lost, the able alchemist can then clothe it in a new form. Likewise when the three principles of an adept (spirit, soul-consciousness, and vital body) are fully integrated we have the liberation of the essential consciousness principle from its imprisonment in form. This is called the Great Perfection.

Plato points out in his *Cratylus* that there is in all things a living essence and it is to this inner nature that the true name of a thing applies.

The greatest and most beautiful passages [of Homer] are those in which he distinguishes between the names that are assigned by men and those that are employed by the Gods.

Throughout the centuries the language of the Mysteries has expressed in many ways. It was used by the Argonauts in their search for the Golden Fleece (body of light). It has been called the Language of the Birds, a veiled reference to the language of the Angels. The Goddess Minerva is said to given it to the prophet Teresias, who passed it on to the great Apollonius of Tyana. Jacob Boehme called it the Language of Nature, which he says

---

[1] *The Hermetic and Alchemical Writings of Paracelsus.* Translated by Arthur Waite. Shambhala Pub. 1976, volumn two, page 318

was taught in the School of Miracles. H.P. Blavatsky called it the 'Mystery Language of the Initiates.'

> There exists, a universal language which an Adept and even a disciple, of any nation may understand by reading it in his own language. . . . In Asia, especially in Devanagri [Sanskrit] characters, every letter had several secret meanings. Interpretations of the hidden sense of such apocalyptic writings are found in the keys given in the Kabalah and they are among its most sacred lore. St. Hieronymus assures us that they were known to the School of the Prophets and were taught therein, which is very likely.[1]

Ragon, the nineteenth century French authority on esoteric Masonry, writes of a time when numbers and letters had a greater significance than they do today.

> *Each of them [numbers and letters] represents by their form a complete sense, which besides the meaning of the word, had a double interpretation adapted to a dual doctrine.*[6]

"This is the language," writes Fulcanelli, "which teaches the mystery of things and unveils the most hidden truths."[7] Iamblichus (250-330 AD), in his profound discourse *On the Mysteries*, writes:

> *I wish to explain to you a form of theology used by the Egyptians to represent the universal and creative principles of the Gods. They expressed invisible concepts through secret mystical symbols in the same way that Nature produces all visible forms from invisible principles.*

This passage not only reveals the truth concerning the secret use of symbols to depict invisible principles, it also, though less obviously perhaps, points to a secret use of symbols. True archetypical symbols

---

[1] H.P. Blavatsky. *The Secret Doctrine* Adyar edition, 1938, vol. 5, p. 118.

[6] *Maconnere Occulte.*

[7] Fulcanelli. *The Mystery of the Cathedrals.*

represent fundamental creative principles. To those students who have developed an esoteric sense and can thus see things in terms of its archetypal energy, these symbols will be understood intuitively. An adept understands these symbols, the truths of nature they represents, and can therefore 'sound' them forth to further the Great Work.

Prima Materia

Before all things the prima materia must be known and applied. Paracelsus

Matter itself is passive and has no motive [causal] faculty of its own at all. We must conclude, therefore, that there is some inward principle that acts upon it and regulates it in all its many aspects of motion. Thomas Vaughn

There abides in nature a certain pure matter, which when discovered and brought by art to perfection, converts to itself proportionally all imperfect bodies that it touches. Arnald di Villanova

There is a celestial, or rather divine water of the chemists, with which both Democritus and Trismegistus were acquainted, calling it divine water, Scythian, etc., which is a spirit of the nature of the ether and quintessence of things, from which the Stone of the Philosophers, takes its beginning. Hermolaus Barbarus

It would be difficult, if not impossible, to obtain a clear understanding of a human being without first looking to the divine spark of life and sentiency hidden within him. So too, it would be difficult to obtain a clear understanding of the nature of alchemy without first discovering that mysterious causal principle that sweeps atoms into organized forms and gives them the life and the impulse to evolve. The Hermetic philosophers called this living force the *Anima Mundi*, the Soul of the Nature. The Pythagoreans and Neo-Platonists called it aether and is now generally known as etheric matter. Paracelsus, the great 16th-century alchemists and physician, called this mysterious substance the alkahest (universal solvent), the invisible element from which all other elements are derived. Thomas Vaughn, the great 17th-century Rosicrucian, alchemist, and mystic seer, called this subtle energy/substance 'the ground of all our secrets.'

> *It is plain that outwardly we see nothing but what is gross—for example earth, water, stones [etc.] . . . All these things have a lumpish, ineffectual outside, but inwardly they are full of a subtle luminosity, impregnated with fire; and this Nature makes use of in generation. Therefore we call it the sperm.*[1]

Jacob Boehme, in his *Mysterium Magnum*, writes:

> *All things of this world have a twofold body, an elemental body, from fire, air, water and earth, and a spiritual body from the astrum;*[2] *one astral [etheric] the other elemental... The sidereal body is higher; the elemental body is only its servant or dwelling-house. The sidereal body dwelleth in the elemental as a world of light in the darkness... Verily the true body is couched in this bestial, gross property; as the gold in the ore.*

---

[1] *Aula Lucis*

[2] Astrum is a Latin term meaning star, glory, and immortal. In early esoteric literature the astrum or astral body refers to the glorious, star-like etheric body, which is immortal.

Isaac Newton, in his new introduction to *The Principia*, which has only recently been published, says that he obtained the inspiration for his theories on gravity and aether from the Pythagoreans.[1] He described aether as the subtle energy field around objects. This, he said, is of several grades from the dense aether around objects to the rare aether around people. He considered aether to be a prime component in his theory of gravity. Many of his great discoveries, most of which were banned from publication by the scientific community, centered around the existence of this very subtle energy field. In a letter to Robert Boyle, the famous chemist, he speaks of changing dense aether into subtle aether, which is basically what alchemy attempts to do.

One of the best books on the subtle energies of the etheric plane obtained through experimental science can be found in Edwin D. Babbitt's monumental classic, *The Principles of Light and Color*. Written in 1878 it is still, in many ways, ahead of its time scientifically. Unfortunately only the scarce original edition is of any value. The editor of the highly abridged University Books reprint, which contains less than half of the original, removed nearly all references to the etheric, because he considered it to be a false concept.

Some scientists claim that aether has been demonstrated to be false. But it is only the specific theory of aether as a medium for light that was demonstrated to be false. Subtle matter and energy still enter into the theories of scientists though of course the names have been changed to protect their prejudices. Scientists now speak about dark matter and dark energy as they once did aether.

Proclus (412-485), who was undoubtedly an initiate of the lesser Mysteries said, "We posses an ethereal body, which not only corresponds to our terrestrial body derived from the four elements, but is analogous to the heavens as well." And in another place he notes; "The whole ethereal sphere imitates the heavens."[2] These two statements show that he not only understood the laws of analogy (as above, so below), but he considered

---

[1] See Joscelyn Godwin's *Harmony of the Spheres*.

[2] Proclus' Commentary on the Timaeus of Plato.

correctly that the etheric sphere to be a direct reflection of the higher worlds.

Master D.K., writing under the name of his student Alice Bailey says:

Esotericism teaches (and modern science is rapidly arriving at the same conclusion) that underlying the physical body and its comprehensive and intricate system of nerves is a vital or etheric body, which is the counterpart and the true form of the outer and tangible phenomenal aspect. It is likewise the medium for the transmission of forces to all parts, for it is itself the repository and the transmitter of energy from the various subjective aspects of man and also from the environment in which man (both inner and outer man) finds himself.[1]

The *lingasharira* of Sanskrit literature describes it as a very complex energy field with centers (*chakras*) and lines of force (*nadies*) through which the subtle etheric energies (*prana*) circulate.

Older alchemical literature seldom mentions the etheric body or subtle energy as it was considered as a part of their secret (esoteric) oral tradition. Those few who understood its meaning veiled it in their writings in various ways. Basil Valentine veiled the secret of the etheric body with the term 'antimony.' In his *The Triumphal Chariot of Antimony,* a veiled treatise on the 'principles of natural bodies,' he says that antimony has two parts. "One is beautiful and pure and of a golden quality containing a considerable amount of Mercury." He also called it the "*Astrum of Sol,* from which all things arise as from the all vivifying sun." 'Astrum' and latter 'astral' is a term that was used in the Mystery Tradition to mean the star like, luminous quality of the etheric plane. H.P. Blavatsky used the term astral plane to mean the etheric plane, but after her death some of her Theosophical followers misunderstood her use of the term, representing it in their writings to mean the desire and emotional plane (*kama*), so that now it is so used. 'Sol' is the sun, the origin of the subtle energy/substance (*prana*) of the etheric plane, which is golden in color.

---

[1] Alice Bailey, *Esoteric Astrology,* page 10.

In the Chinese alchemical classic, *The Secret of the Golden Flower*, the highly refined and energized etheric body at a level of development reflecting spiritual energy from above is referred to as the 'Golden Flower.' In Greek mythology it was called the 'Golden Fleece.' In the *Book of Revelation* by St. John and in the *Chemical Wedding* by Christian Rosencreutz, the founder of the original Rosicrucians, the purified luminous state (*ultima materia*) of the etheric body is called 'the wedding garment' and 'clothed in white garments.'

The energy that circulates throughout the vital body of any living organism and gives it its life and vitality has, over the centuries, been given many names— prana, *vita spiritus*, chi, psi, odic force, etc. Prana, the etheric bodies through which it flows, and the complete all encompassing etheric sphere, are united in essence with the one universal subtle energy field, sometimes called the *akashic* web, from which all living organisms arise.

In the early esoteric literature of both the East and the West the term most often used to indicate, and at the same time to conceal, the etheric energy-substance, the *prima materia*, is 'water.' H.P. Blavatsky points out in her *Secret Doctrine* that "'Waters' and 'water' stand as a symbol for Akasha the Primordial Ocean of Space..."[1] Raymund Lully, writing of the term 'water' as used in alchemical literature says.

> *It is not water but earth that is pregnant with the sun.... It is the prima materia or first matter, the substance of which our stone is made.*

In the *Book of Genesis* (1-2) it is written: "And the vital breath [*anima mundi*] of the Elohim[2] moved upon the face of the Waters." The Greek philosopher Theophrustus writes: "Water nourishes the sun and the stars, and even the whole of cosmos." Jianine Miller, in her illuminating and overlooked book, *The Vision of Cosmic Order in the Cosmos*, writes of the term 'water' as it was used in the Vedas of ancient India:

---

[1] Adyar edition, volume II, page 177.

[2] The term Elohim is plural and therefore cannot be translated simply as God as it was in the King James translation. The term may have originated from the Egyptian Aleim, meaning the powerful ones or gods.

The waters are the primordial substance, the original state of matter of which all things are shaped in the depths of space to manifest finally through the more concrete element, earth. . . . The Watery abyss, the Great Mother, the Chaos of the Greeks, the Great Deep of Genesis, is not only the primeval protomateria out of which all the universe is fashioned, but also the womb wherein is hidden the elixir of immortality.[1]

The Hindus called it *Akasha*, the 'Waters of Space.' The Persians called it the 'Water of Life.' To the Hebrews it was *Ain Sophi*. The Taoists called it *Hun-tan*, the primordial chaos. It is undoubtedly the 'dark matter' and 'dark energy' of the physicist. When the alchemist say, "the first work is to reduce the body into water, and that this is called solution, which is the foundation of the Hermetic art" it means that one must first reduce the elements back into their original astral condition. The author of *Rosarium Philosohorum* states:

The first preparation and foundation of the Hermetic Art is solution and a reduction of the body into water, which is argent vive (vital and alive); for it is well known to artists that species cannot as themselves, be transmuted. The philosophers have said our stone is made of one thing, and that is true. Complete mastery is accomplished with our water, which is the sperm of all metals and as we have said all metals are resolved into it.

That something cannot be transmuted as itself means that it must be first reduced to it essential nature.

Mary Atwood, in her brilliant 1850 alchemical masterpiece, *A Suggestive Inquiry into the Hermetic Mystery*, plainly reveals publically one of the primary secrets of the Art:

---

[1] Page 75

When Hermes says that the separation of the ancient philosophers is made upon water, dividing it into four substances, it is not common water to which he alludes.... It is the ethereal body of life and light.[3]

As we have stated one of ways to decipher early alchemical literature is to translate the symbolic key words as to their higher or lower correspondences. For example, the four elements of the early Hermetic philosophers—earth, water, air, and fire—were used in esoteric literature to not only represent oxygen, hydrogen, nitrogen and carbon, but also their higher correspondences, the four grades of etheric substance. In *The Golden Treatise of Hermes* it is stated:

Understand, O Sons of Wisdom that knowledge of the four elements of the ancient philosophers cannot be found corporally. They can only be discovered by patiently looking to their causes, which are hidden.

The Hermetic Mysteries, which can be traced to the Ancient Mysteries of both the East and the West, taught that the corporal material universe arose from hidden causes emanating from the *prima materia* (subtle etheric matter). Hermes here instructs the students to look for the hidden causes, the source and essence of matter. The alchemist works not with dense matter but with the etheric matter behind it through the creative activity of psychic energy.

Djwhal Khul and Rudolf Steiner, both initiates of the White Brotherhood, have divided the physical plane into the seven subplanes— solid, liquid, gaseous, and four levels of etheric substance. Brother D.K lists them as follows:

1. First ether
2. Second ether
3. Third ether
4. Fourth ether

---

3 Page 95.

5. Gas
6. Liquid
7. Solid

Rudolf Steiner divides them in a similar way:

1. Life ether.
2. Sound-ether
3. Light-ether
4. Fire-ether
5. Air
6. Water
7. Earth

Thomas Vaughn, a direct disciple of an initiate of the Rosicrucian Brotherhood, says that first matter is 'the quintessence of four,' meaning the four etheric elements. Georg Von Welling (1652–1727), also a follower of the Rosicrucian Brotherhood, writes in his alchemical classic *Opus Mago-Cabbalisticum et Theosophicum* that the four elements of earth, water, air and fire were generally used in alchemical treatises to represent the 'four invisible elements.' He gives the secret glyphs for these elements as follows:

The element of fire, both visible and invisible, is considered to be two aspects (higher and lower) of the one fire subplane of the seven-fold physical/etheric plane. The higher correspondence of this fiery element is manas (mind) higher and lower. Von Welling, speaking symbolically, says

---

[1] See Von Welling's *Opus Mago-Cabbalisticum et Theosophicum*, page 53. Weiser Books, 2006, Translated by Joseph G. McVeigh.

that the four invisible elements are the four heavenly streams of the River of Life that originates in Eden. This stream, he tells us, arises from the Sea of Glass and Fire spoken of in the *Book of Revelation*. Eden, as I have indicated in my work, *The Apocalypse of St. John*, is a reference to the etheric plane. Brother D.K. hinted at this in his *A Treatise on Cosmic Fire,* when he said that the mythic Garden of Eden is the planetary etheric center that absorbs the vital subtle energy of the sun for distribution to all earthly organisms, including the earth itself.[1]

According to Paracelsus there is a big difference between *prima materia* (first matter) and *ultima materia* (perfected matter). The latter is geometrically represented by the pentagram ☆ or from another perspective the triangular cubic stone—manifesting 'four square.'

---

[1] Alice Bailey, *A Treatise on Cosmic Fire*, page 84.

T

The Transmutation of Physical Substance

Only thought can act upon the primary substance.
Heart

Ivan G. McDaniel, in his illuminating Rosicrucian work, *Lamp of the Soul*, reveals an important alchemical secret:

Atoms brought in contact with lights of a certain frequency become disturbed and expand. Atoms which have settled down are spoken of as being in their stable state, and when disturbed as being in an excited state. The sparks in electrical discharges and the glow in vacuum tubes are excited atoms reorganizing their electrons and at the same time throwing out excess energy in the form of light frequency. After such an impulse the electrons fall back into the original state, but the atom continues to emit radiation of a certain frequency. This energy that the atoms throw off is available for organization into new patterns provided the positive center is established around which the electrons may function. In psychogenesis the atomic structure of the body is vitalized by raising up forces from certain parts of the body and the emitted energy is drawn to the Soul center and there blended with the soul essence in the formulation of the individual soul.[1]

---

[1] Page 34, Philosophical Pub, 1942.

One of the primary secrets of alchemy is given veiled in the final sentence of the above quotation. The term 'psychogenesis' when used in conjunction with matter pertains to its psychic origin. It is psychic energy, the creative power of thought, that raises the frequency of the atoms involved to a point where radiation-transmutation occurs. From this we see that the transmutation of one element into another need not be accomplished, as nuclear scientists do now, by bombarding the nucleus with so-called fast particles. The 'lights' used to raise the frequency of the atoms are subtle and are not normally visible except to one with etheric vision. The 'soul center' here is the nucleus of the atom. The 'soul essence' is the central spark. It is in the establishing the positive center is where many alchemists of the past have failed. Without a hermetically sealed etheric field to contain the central spark it is invariably lost.

After the electrons are disturbed they may not continue to revolve at just any chance distance form the nucleus of the atom. There are certain prescribed distances called energy levels, any one of which the electrons may occupy but the intervening spaces between these levels are zones of instability in which the electrons may not remain but through which they may pass. This shifting of the electrons from one level to another is responsible for the emission of energy. The law governing the motion of electrons in atoms is known as wave mechanics. These levels of energy interpenetrate one another so that at a given point and with proper knowledge it would be possible to exchange atoms from one level for those of another level, and by doing so change the character of the organism in which the exchange is made.

Physical alchemy can be applied to either organic or inorganic substance. Biological alchemy, which is primarily applied to regeneration and the healing arts, is the more important of the two. The principles of psychogenesis and wave mechanics apply to both approaches.

Some Hermetic philosophers maintain that the primary mission of humanity (The Great Work) involves the spiritualization (perfection) of matter (*ultima materia*). This involves the elevation and transmutation of dense matter into a higher more exalted state. This is consistent with the idea, as taught in all esoteric schools of merit, that the evolutionary process, call is destiny or God's will, moves all the kingdoms of nature from a lower to a more refined or exalted state. Paracelsus noted:

> *Nothing has been created as the ultima materia, its final state. Everything is first created in its prima materia, its primordial substance; whereupon Vulcan comes and by an act of alchemy develops it into its final substance.*[1]

The Evolution of Nature is a long slow process culminating at the end of each epoch, each great cyclic progression, in the transmutation of the old forms of that cycle into those new and subtler forms that are more in harmony with its new elevated level of being. Vulcan is Nature's Blacksmith. With his hammer he welds the creative power of the spiritual will, according to the currents of that evolution. The fire of Vulcan is psychic energy. According to Basil Valentine, "the Artist and Vulcan must agree." This means that the will of the alchemist must be in step with the currents of evolution. Vulcan draws forth with his hammer (the Tau T) fiery sparks from the heart of matter and unites them with their higher counterpart. It is this Chemical Wedding, which when applied to the physical plane, initiates the natural transmutation of material substance.

Ultima materia, as Hermes tells us, is matter (energy-substance) that that has evolved full circle from the invisible *prima materia* down into the extreme density of the visible universe, and back again to its original primordial state, with added and refined qualities gained from the process. Master D.K. in his *A Treatise on Cosmic Fire*, a book which was written primarily for initiates, states:

> *Intangible objective substance has been condensed into the tangible objective world. This—under the evolutionary plan—has to be again*

---

[1] Labyrinthus medicorum errantium. Quoted in *Paracelsus: Selected Writings*. Edited by Jolande Jacob. Bollingen Series XXVIII, page 215.

transmuted into its original condition, plus the gain of ordered rhythm and the tendencies and qualities wrought in the consciousness of its atoms and elements through the experience of externalization.[1]

Alchemy, which follows the natural cyclic evolutionary activity of nature, is essentially a two-part, two-directional process; abstraction ↑ and externalization ↓. In alchemical terms this is called 'volatilized matter' and 'fixing the volatile.' First, through the power of Vulcan and the creative application of psychic energy, the alchemists must abstract the vital essence from the form without losing it and unite it with its higher counterpart. This is the transmutation of its essential nature into its original condition. He must then create a subtle sheath into which the vital essence is to be contained and through which it must later descend, to be externalized or fixed, to take on a new and more subtle form than before. Abstract and manifest, dissolve and congeal, purify and calcify, dematerialize and materialize, evolution and involution, death and rebirth all refer to this fundamental cycle ebb and flow of the evolutionary process, the great in-breath and out-breath of Life. Says the exalted Teacher:

Manvantaras and Pralayas [the manifestation and abstraction of the universe] can be discerned in everything. Definitely from the tiniest manifestation to a change of worlds this majestic law can be seen.[2]

"Transmutation," writes D.K., "is the changing of one vibration and one vibratory activity into another higher one." Lead, say the alchemists, is low on the evolutionary scale of the mineral kingdom, while gold is high. Therefore by raising the vibratory activity of lead to a higher vibratory frequency gold can be created. How, you might ask, do we change the vibrational activity of something? First we must remember that etheric matter (and all matter is etheric at its core) is a pattern of energy held in place by a life force of some kind. The vibrational activity of this pattern of energy is changed by stimulating its life force, its central core, into greater

---

[1] Alice Bailey. *A Treatise on Cosmic Fire.* N.Y. 1925.

[2] Agni Yoga Society. *Heart.*

activity. This is accomplished by what the old alchemists called 'a projection of the stone.' This stimulates the etheric seeds to a point where radiation naturally begins to occur. In this way its keynote can be changed (raised) and the outer form, which no longer matches the new rate of vibration, disintegrates. It is here that the exiting 'heavenly flyer' needs to be quickly captured, isolated, and 'hermetically sealed' in its own 'ring pass not.' It is here, we are told,[1] that many alchemist fail and the Phoenix rising from the ashes, instead of manifesting into a new form, escapes to the cosmic reservoir of primordial substance. The projection of the stone is accomplished through the direct application of the alchemical fire.

Most of the Adepts agree that for transmutation to be successful we must follow the same steps and processes that Nature Herself follows. Solomon Trismosin stressed this in his alchemical masterpiece *Splendor Solis*. When transmutation occurs in nature, as in radioactive material, for example, it is the nuclear particles escaping as radiation that cause the form to disintegrate and not the reverse. In other words, as we have stated, we cannot extract the essential particles from the elements simply by consuming them in fire or melting the metals down to a liquid mass.

We know from the discoveries made in physics at the beginning of the 20th-century that matter is transmuted into energy when the particles involved increase their vibratory activity, their velocity in mass, to a point where they equal the speed of light.[2] The process of this etherialization of dense matter happens naturally in radioactive substances. It can be produced artificially by the alchemist by stimulating the inner essence or nucleus of the atoms with what Eliphas Levi called the universal dissolvent.

> *The force of this dissolvent is concentrated in the quintessence —that is to say, at the equilibrating center of a dual polarity. The four elements of the ancients are the four forces of the universal magnet, represented by the figure of the cross, which revolves indefinitely about its own center and so propounds the enigma represented by the quadrant of the circle.*[4]

---

[1] Alice Bailey, *A Treatise on Cosmic Fire,* page 494.
[2] See Ernest Rutherford. *The Transmutation of Matter.* The Royal Institution 1930
[4] Levi. *The History of Magic* p. 364

"The Rod of Initiation," says the Teacher, "is for the human kingdom what the Philosopher's Stone is for the alchemist."[1] In other words there is a close correspondence between the process of Initiation into the Mysteries, which involves the transformation of the consciousness through the application of the Flaming Diamond (the Rod of Initiation) and the transmutation of physical substance through the application of the Philosopher's Stone. In both cases the electromagnetic stimulation increases the vibrational activity of the essential atoms involved to a point of the exodus of the central spark.

Rudolf Steiner writes:

To be initiated means that faculties slumbering in every human soul are awakened. These faculties enable a person to look into the spiritual world that exists behind our physical world.

Thomas Vaughn, states:

The Anima Mundi [the central spark] is confined and imprisoned by lawful magic in a liquid crystal [etheric form]. The light, which is in her, streams through the water [ether] and is made visible to the [clairvoyant] eye. In this state it is made subject to the artist.

The agent of transmutation, the alchemical fire, is always of a finer subtler grade than the substance being transmuted. The secret fire of the alchemists is psychic energy, which the alchemist develops first by mastering their own nature, and then as an extension of this, by mastering the elements. To master this energy the alchemist is encouraged to experiment first in the plant kingdom, where the effects can be readily perceived. When the creative power of psychic energy is realized we will understand that the forces of alchemy extend far beyond what we usually think of as the laws of physical nature.

---

[1] *Heart* 27

The true forces of nature are to be found in the subtle world of mind, soul and spirit. And while this is contrary to the thinking of material minded scientists it is nevertheless true. Even when applied to the natural processes of the body, such as digestion and respiration, their inner activity extends far beyond that which can be detected or measured by material instruments. Only the trained clairvoyant seer perceives directly the causes behind their physical activity.

The secret alchemical fire is applied through a projection of Vulcan. The crucible is made of subtle matter. And when the etheric form, along with its gaseous sheath, is completed, it will, through the Law of Attraction, naturally precipitate itself into physical manifestation.

Wolf D. Storl, in his excellent book on Biodynamic Gardening, *Culture and Horticulture,* states that the aim of alchemy is "to permeate matter with form-giving spirit, and to provide spirit with substance." He is here pointing out two natural and fundamental processes, involution (↓) and evolution (↑) as they apply to alchemy.

Creation-involution (↓) involves the 3 fold *prima materia* △ plus the 4 elements ☐ equals the sevenfold field of manifestation

Evolution-transmutation (↑) involves the sevenfold field plus the central spark ◡ minus the three fold Maya ▽ equals the *ultima materia* ✪ . The intense fire of the manifesting central spark burns away the dense outer shell or maya leaving perfected matter on one level and a perfected adept on another.

Projecting the Stone involves  plus equals or

The six pointed star with a point at its center represents not only the seven subplanes of the physical (or any) plane, but 'on a higher turn of the spiral,' the seven planes in total.

Maya in the human kingdom manifests through the three-fold personality (the physical body, the feeling nature (*kama*), and the reasoning mind (lower *manas*). The three together refer to the not-self. On the seven fold physical plane maya is the three lowest subplanes: gas, liquid, and solid, or air, water, and earth.

Radiation

Having attained the state of the Sun and Moon, one
illuminates the corners of the world with the light of one's
own body.   Nagarjuna

In the early 20th century it was successfully demonstrated by scientists that radioactivity was a natural process involving the spontaneous transmutation of matter into energy. According to Einstein's famous equation $E=mc^2$, a tremendous amount of energy is generated through the transmutation of a very small amount of matter. Master D.K., in his *A Treatise on Cosmic Fire*, a book which Albert Einstein once checked out of a library in New York City,[1] says that the Law of Radiation, which governs the transmutation process, operates according to fixed laws that apply equally to all the kingdoms of nature.

Radiation is the outer effect produced by all forms in all kingdoms when
their internal activity has reached such a stage of vibratory activity that the
confining walls of the form no longer form a prison, but permit of the escape
of the subjective essence. It marks a specific point of attainment in the

---

[1] Lucis Trust Lending Library.

evolutionary process and this is equally true of the atom of substance with which the chemist and physicist deal, when working with the elements, as it is of the forms in the vegetable kingdom, the forms of the animal kingdom, in the human, and likewise in the divine.[1]

Due to the radiance of its inner essence, the eucalyptus tree, for example, is esoterically regarded as radioactive.[2] In the human kingdom the radiation of light produced from the regeneration of the physical/etheric body is sometimes seen emanating from the auras of highly developed saints and sages. The radioactivity of the physical body is brought about by an increase in the vibratory activity of the etheric body as a whole, which arises from an increase in the vibratory rate of an illuminated mind. Whatever takes place in the consciousness is directly reflected in kind in the etheric body and eventually in the dense physical body as well. As the consciousness is illuminated the energy-substance of the vehicles (physical/etheric, emotional, and mental) are thereby equally illuminated, even to the point of eventually illuminating the body with a radiant and a subtle light. J. Todd Ferrier in his masterwork *Life's Mysteries Unveiled* states that the radiation of the human faculties takes place through Living Waters that stream in to us from the heights in response to the love we generate.

Divine Love can accomplish all things. It can change the will and make the soul as radiant as a child of the radiant-heavens. It can make the intuition so clear in its perception that it misunderstands not, but cometh to know all things. It can transfuse the etheric body and make of it a body of glorious radiance, which inwardly pours itself in adoration before the Divine, and outwardly creates the atmosphere by which the child of God should ever be encompassed. It can even touch the body of the outermost and transform its substances, purifying and revivifying its life-stream until even the transfiguration of Being in the innermost pours its radiance through the outermost.

---

[1] Alice Bailey, *A Treatise on Cosmic Fire*, Page 1060.

[2] Alice Bailey, *A Treatise on Cosmic Fire*, Page 1064

The Teacher, and author of the Agni Yoga Books, said:

There is a state of development of psychic energy called luminous, and a being at this stage begins to emit light. . . . First we see the outer light, then that [light which is] within ourselves and only after kindling of the 'torch' [of the heart] can we radiate light.[1]

The radiation and eventual regeneration of the human vehicles occur only after the fire of the heart has been kindled. All subtle energies within the etheric body must pass through and be purified by the fire of the heart. It eventually transmutes the subtle energies of the etheric body to a point where first radiation and then complete transfiguration of the body and mind occurs. Brother D.K. said:

Radiation is transmutation in process of accomplishment. Transmutation being the liberation of the essence in order that it may seek a new centre.... Basically it is the result of the inner positive nucleus of force or life reaching such a terrific rate of vibration, that it eventually scatters the electrons or negative points that compose its sphere of influence and scatters them to such a distance that the Law of Repulsion dominates. The atomic sphere, if I might so express it, dissipates, the electrons come under the Law of Repulsion and the central essence escapes and seeks a new sphere, occultly understood.[2]

The Law of Repulsion is the natural inclination of matter when separated from the central core, which through the Law of Attraction holds it together. This process is also applicable on a higher turn of spiral to a human being and the transmutation/radiation of the body.

The dark light of the tiny atoms of which the physical vehicle is constructed is responsive to the stimulation passing down from the soul into its vehicle, and, when man is under the control of the soul, there eventuates the shining forth of the light throughout the body. This shows as the radiance emanating from the

---

[1] *Heart.* # 38
[2] Alice Bailey, *A Treatise on Cosmic Fire* p. 478

bodies of adepts and saints, giving the effect of a bright and shining light. When the light of the soul is blended with the magnetic light of the vital body, it stimulates the atoms of the physical body to such an extent that each atom becomes in turn a tiny radiant centre. This only becomes possible when the head, heart, and solar plexus and the centre at the base of the spine are connected in a peculiar fashion, which is one of the secrets of initiation.[3]

The alchemical wedding, which is often mentioned in alchemical texts as being necessary before transmutation can take place, pertains to the union of positive and negative energies. In the human kingdom this unification is between the soul and body. This causes the descent of the spiritual Light. St. Seraphim, the Russian Orthodox saint, called the accumulation of the spiritual light, 'the acquisition of the Holy Spirit,' which he says 'is the true aim of the Christian life.' He demonstrated this acquisition to his disciple Motovilov, who described what he saw in some detail:

After these words I glanced at his face and there came over me an even greater reverent awe. Imagine in the center of the sun, in the dazzling light of its midday rays, the face of the man talking to you. You see the movement of his lips and the changing expression of his eyes, you hear his voice, you feel someone holding your shoulders; yet, you do not see his hands, you do not even see yourself or his figure, but only a blinding light spreading far around for several yards and illuminating with its sheen both the snow blanket which covered the forest glade and the snow-flakes which besprinkled me and the great Elder. You can imagine the state I was in![4]

St. Seraphim listed some of the signs that accompany the acquisition of the Holy Spirit:

---

[3] Alice Bailey. *A Treatise on White Magic*. N.Y. 1934, pp 105 & 106.

[4] N.A. Motovilov. *The Aquisition of the Holy Spirit*, quoted in Archimandrite Moore's *St. Seraphim of Sorov*, Chapter VIII.

1. A calmness and peace of the soul. "This is the peace of which the Lord said, 'my peace I give to you which is not the peace which the world gives.'

2. An extraordinary joy in the heart. "When the Spirit comes down to man and overshadows him with the fullness of His descent, then the human soul overflows with unspeakable joy, for the Spirit of God fills with joy whatever it touches."

3. An extraordinary warmth. "By it the hermits of both sexes were kept warm and did not fear the winter frost, being clad, as in fur coats, in the grace-giving clothing woven by the Holy Spirit."

In the Agni Yoga Teachings some of the signs accompanying the descent of the spiritual Light include:

> *Someone heard far off voices; someone envisioning it, participated in the Subtle World; someone became luminous; someone levitated, someone walked on water; someone could read thoughts; someone could read with closed eyes a closed book; someone swallowed poison without harm; someone did not feel pain; someone in the snow generated the heat of the heart; someone did not feel fatigue; someone could help by healing; someone could manifest knowledge of the future. Thus, one can enumerate all the manifested phenomena and a multitude of instructive examples from life. But for an instant gather all these qualities into one body and you will have the new human transmutation indicated in many Teachings.*[5]

An ancient fragment from the *Old Commentary*, translated by Brother D.K., states:

> *The Solar Orb shines forth in radiant splendor.*
> *The illuminated mind reflects the solar glory.*
> *The lunar orb rises from the centre to the summit,*
> *When the three suns are one, Brahma breaks forth.*
> *And a lighted world is born.*

---

[5] *Heart # 99*

'D.K. gives an interesting commentary on this ancient fragment.

This literally means, that when the soul (symbolized by the Solar Orb) the mind and the light in the head form a single unit, the creative power of the Solar Angel can express itself in the three worlds, and can construct a form through which its energy can actively express itself.[6]

The 'three suns' represent the three fires of the etheric body, which are direct reflections of the creative fire of the mind, the wisdom fire of the heart, and the dynamic fire of the will. (We will cover the 'three fires' further in later chapter) Through their unification (the alchemical wedding) Brahma, the third or mother aspect of the Hindu Trinity and the Holy Spirit of the Christians, 'breaks forth' (is released) as intense radiation of the creative fire, Shakti, the inner life, behind all manifested life.

The 'absorption and radiation of the light', whether of a sun, an atom, or the human organism, is a great mystery. Brother D.K. gives this hint:

Initiation veils a secret and the revelation of the secret is imminent. Just what this secret is, I may not reveal, but it is concerned with a peculiar type of energy, which can be induced at a moment of supreme tension. The only possible hint I can give you in connection with this mysterious matter is that it is closely related to the 'Blinding Light,' which Saul of Tarsus saw on the road to Damascus and the 'blinding light,' which accompanied the discharge of energy from the atomic bomb . . . . The 'principle of absorption' of the light emerges as one of the subjects to be studied, understood and mastered between initiations, for each initiation carries the subject another step forward.[8]

---

[6] Alice Bailey. *A Treatise on White Magic.* p. 98

[8] Alice Bailey. *Discipleship in the New Age.*

Transmutation of Psychic Energy

ne O of the primary secrets of the esoteric Mysteries, one that is now being discovered by the alternative healing community, is the truth that *whatever happens in the consciousness is directly reflected in the etheric body and thus by reflex the dense physical body.* Thus psychic energy, the energy generated by our thoughts and feelings, directly effect the etheric centers, which in turn produces changes in the chemistry of the dense physical body, via the glandular system. It is for this reason that the health of the body can often be traced directly to one's thoughts and feelings. *As we raise and refine the consciousness corresponding energies in the etheric body also are raised, and as a result transmuted to a higher more refined state of energy.* This evolutionary process takes place naturally in everyone, though it only becomes a fully conscious activity toward the end of our long pilgrimage through the physical plane.

Briefly stated the emotional and desire energies that are generated within the astral body are over many lifetimes refined, purified, and transmuted into the pure feelings of the heart—love and wisdom. This transmutation of the psychic energy of the feeling consciousness is directly reflected in the etheric body as the transmutation of the energies of the solar-plexus center upward to the heart center and from there to twelve petalled Brahmarandhara center at the top of the head sometimes called the 'heart in the head.' At each station a portion of the energy is transmuted into a higher more refined state.

The transmutation of the creative energy of thought on the mental plane is reflected in the etheric body and producing thereby the transmutation of the creative energy of the sacral center into the higher creative activity of throat and ajna centers. The evolution and transmutation of the energies of the etheric centers from the lower to the higher centers is the direct result of corresponding activity of the psychic energies of the mental and astral planes. The Adepts always work form above down. Physical energies and influence the mental plane but it cannot control it. Physical energies can be, and should be, controlled by thought.

These two stream of pranic energy eventually become the two primary reflections in the etheric body, yin and yang, of a refined and purified feeling and mental consciousness. They ascend through two etheric channels called the *ida* and *pingala*, moving in a spiral fashion around the central channel, the *axis mundi* of the spinal column (*sushumna*) and are eventually synthesized at the crown.

When these two currents of energy are synthesized in the head, and personal will, which is reflected in the center at the base of the spine, is in the process of being transmuted into spiritual will, the energy of that center also begins to rise. This happens naturally as the spiritual will is developed and should not be attempted through visualization. The primary rule of self development is that the Path is always to be trod naturally (Natural here means in step with the Tao). Nothing on the Way should be forced or artificially manipulated. The energies of the etheric body naturally follow the activity of our psychic energy, the creative power of the mind. Master the thoughts and feelings and the centers will develop naturally and accordingly.

When the subtle pranic energy that corresponds with the human will has enters the central channel we have a direct correspondence to the 'Nobel Middle Path' that willfully steers a middle course upward between the extremes of the pair of opposites. This symbolism, says Master D.K, "is a miniature picture of the whole evolution of spirit and matter."[1] When the creative mind find perfect equilibrium with the love/wisdom of the heart, the Middle Path, which leads between the 'pairs of opposites' to the supreme truth of Unity, can be found and followed. The unity of the three fires of the body takes place only as a reflection of a corresponding unity of the three fires of consciousness, where the perceiver[2], that which is perceived,[3] and the act of perceiving[4], are one and the same.

[1] *A Treatise on Cosmic Fire, page 1159*
[2] Vishyi.
[3] Vishaya.
[4] Sambandha.

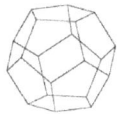

The Philosopher's Stone

The Philosopher's Stone [is] that effective transmuting agent which will bring about revelation and the power to impose the will of the chemist upon the elemental forces, which work in, by and through matter. Master D.K.

The Philosopher's Stone should regenerate man no less than metals. Paracelsus

For those who understand how to use the Philosopher's Stone, death occurs in appearance only. Rudolf Steiner

There never was in all eternity anything more precious than this Stone. It is offered by God and is bestowed upon man. Everyone may have it that doth desire it. It is in a most simple form and hath the power of Deity in it. Jacob Boehme

The symbol of the Philosopher's Stone can be interpreted on several levels, all of which involves to the crystallization of subtle energies. The only difference being the degree of crystallization, the subtlety of energy and the plane or level upon which the manifestation is to take place. Transmutation is essentially the abstraction of the volatile life essence from a living body so that it may be clothed in a new, more refined, form. The manifestation of the Philosopher's Stone proceeds in the opposite direction. It involves the descent and materialization of subtle energies. This is sometimes called 'fixing the volatile'. When applied to a human being it represents the natural and spontaneous precipitation and crystallization of spiritual energies within the vajra (etheric) body.

> *The Philosopher's Stone is something real. It must be understood spiritually and physically. The spiritual condition that is called 'Stone' corresponds to the consonance of all precipitates of psychic energy. Physically the preparation is quite close to the preparation of Paracelsus, but he made a basic error on which he insisted in vain. As for the rest, the Arabian sources that sustained Paracelsus were quite correct.*[1]

The key words here are 'precipitates of psychic energy.' The Philosopher's Stone is a condensation for the manifestation in the physical/etheric world of the astral light, the radiant energy/substance of the subtle world. According to Paracelsus this vital essence (*primum ens*) can be found in and extracted from the certain herbs for the making of powerful subtle medicines. The Adept when applying alchemical principles, even on the physical plane, will make use of psychic energy. We will examine Paracelsus' work on the Philosopher's Stone later. His basic error may have been his insistence that something could be created from nothing. One of the primary Arabian sources that sustained Paracelsus may have been Jabir ibn Hayyan (Geber). His work is highly veiled.

Jacob Boehme lightly veils the secret of the Philosopher's Stone in a letter to his student Sbraham of Sommerfeld:

> *I am assured that the Lord will open to you the door of His love in the mystery and **crown** you with the **diadem** of His wisdom, which is more precious than the created heaven of this world. For the precious philosopher's stone, the ground of all mysteries **doth lie therein**. And this same diadem is beset with this stone, which the soul puts on **as a garment**, being a new body in and for the Kingdom of God. This diadem is pure with divine beauty. It gladdens the heart in its afflictions. It goes along with man into death, but has no death in it. It liveth eternal as a guide to heaven and the joy of angels. He that obtains it esteems it higher*

---

[1] *Heart* 27

*than all the goods and riches of the world. It groweth in tribulation and affliction, but it is harvested with great joy. Such **a crown is set upon** him that seeketh after it with earnestness, but not in the self-reason of flesh and blood, as my writings testify. For what is therein written the author hath known by experience. There is no strange hand or spirit behind my writings.*[1]

Key words in this passage include the hints 'diadem' and 'crown'. It is interesting that Jacob Boehme, like his modern counterpart Rudolf Steiner, did not 'channel' his work, but rather wrote from experience.

When the Rosicrucians say that the Philosopher's Stone is 'condensed light, contained and fixed about a centre' they are speaking literally. The descent and crystallization of the volatile essence they called 'a deposit of light.' In the Vajrayana scriptures there are two Sanskrit terms that represent the crystallization of the light in the vajra (etheric) body depending upon its degree of condensation and its level of manifestation— the *murdhajoytish*, which literally means 'light *(joyish)* at the summit' *(murdhan)* and the *abasabindu*, which means 'clear light *(abasa)* at the center point of tension *(bindu).*' The first appearance of this manifesting light is as the *murdhajoytish*. Patanjali in his *Yoga Sutras*, 3:32, writes of this light: "Through one-pointed concentration upon the light in the head *(murdhajoytish)* a vision of the perfected ones can be attained." To "contain and fix the spiritual light about a center" is accomplished by "holding the mind steady in the light."

"The personality hides within itself," writes Master D.K., "as a casket hides a jewel, that point of soul light which we call the light in the head."[12] Vajrayana scriptures call this light a 'shining jewel,' as it is a direct reflection of the clear light of an illuminated consciousness.

The author of *The Secret Symbols of the Rosicrucians*, Hinricus Theosophus, in his *Golden Treatise on the Philosopher's Stone* states correctly that in the creation of the Philosopher's Stone nature herself does all the work. The alchemist may hasten the process by removing the obstacles

---

1

12 Bailey. *A Treatise on White Magic.*

and by drawing, through the law of attraction, the incoming energies to a "point of tension" through the power of Vulcan, but nature does the rest

"Anything in nature that can form a crystallized deposit from a solution," writes Rudolf Steiner, "was called 'salt' by the Rosicrucian of the Middle Ages."[1] Hinricus Theosophus continues:

> *The good hearted follower of our art is many times sufficiently instructed, not only as to where our Materia should be obtained but also that it is a single Materia which, through the skill of the artist is dissolved into two aspects, vis., into water and earth.*

When the clear light of the *Materia Lucida* (radiant substance) is dissolved or absorbed into water we have Soma, the 'hidden Manna,' the divine 'elixir of immortality' and the 'crystalline due.' When crystallized into earth we have the much sought after 'Philosopher's Stone,' which in the East was called the 'Wish-fulfilling Gem,' because of its power to intensify and manifest the creative power of psychic energy. The quality and potency of the 'Stone' depends upon the quality and potency of the psychic energy being condensed as well as the tension of Vulcan and ability of the artist.

> *The heart governs psychic energy. The crystal can multiply its forces, which is saturated with fiery energy. In striving to compress psychic energy one should discern subtly which impulses actually create [it]. Because upon the quality of the impulse will depend the tension of psychic energy. Thus, fearlessness and fiery striving for achievement will produce crystals of psychic energy. These crystals are soluble with difficulty, for they consist of the most fiery substances. Therefore, manifestations of the fiery centers can be revealed only to the spirit which knows fearlessness and the power of fiery aspiration toward achievement.[2]*

The 'crystals of psychic energy,' which contains 'the fiery substance' and condensation of light, is our Philosopher's Stone.

---

[1] Rudolf Steiner, *The Secret Stream   Christian Rosenkreutz and Rosicrucianism,* Anthroposophic Press 2000, page 140.
[2] *Fiery World,* Volume III # 421.

One of the ways in which the ancient alchemists veiled the hidden purpose of alchemy was by stating that its purpose was to make gold, though they would sometimes hint that it was not common gold they were referring to but Hermetic gold. In this regard Robert Fludd (1574-1637), a student of the true and original Rosicrucians, gives the following veiled hint:

> *Hermetic gold is the outflow of the sunbeam, or of light suffused invisibly and magically into the body of the world. Light is sublimated gold, rescued magically by invisible stellar attraction, out of material depths. Gold is thus the deposit of light, which of itself generates. Light in the celestial world is subtle, vaporous, magically exalted gold, or 'spirit of flame.' Gold draws inferior natures in the metals, and intensifying and multiplying, converts into itself.[1]*

This beautiful statement, which will appear as nonsense to many, does not conflict with the physics of Einstein that proclaims both light and matter to be energy vibrating at different degrees of intensity. Gold (in fact all matter) is indeed "a deposit of light," and light is gold (or any matter), transmuted to a higher frequency. Hermetic gold, so called to distinguish it from common gold, is the condensation of the spiritual light into *materia lucida*, or subtle matter that is radiant with golden light. In the last analysis light is a subtle matter that is radiant with energy.

"The Philosopher's Stone," says Mary Atwood in her alchemical masterpiece *A Suggestive Inquiry into the Hermetic Mystery,* "is a real entity produced by spiritual generation. It is a real *ens* [essence] of light." The Stone is not a poetic abstraction but rather something real and even tangible. That Atwood knew the secret of the Philosopher's Stone, both in the general and specific sense, and even where it was to be found, is demonstrated in the following cleverly worded hint that she gave in her commentary on *The Golden Treatise* of Hermes Trismegistus.

> *He [Hermes] who should have received so much **grace** from the Father of Light, as to obtain in this life the inestimable gift of the*

---

[1] *The Rosicrucians,* by Robertus di Fluctibus. Quoted in H.P. Blavatsky's *Isis Unveiled* Vol. 1 page 511

Philosopher's Stone; who carries it about with him, even in his own breast, the treasury of universal nature.[1]

In another place she says: "This process takes place in and through the human body in the blood."

H. Curtiss hints at this in her masterpiece on esoteric numbers, *The Key of Destiny*, by H. Curtiss, page 268:

All the chemical elements of the Philosopher's Stone found in the universe, are also to be found in the body of man, even in the literal sense, that is, as chemical elements.

And in the *Rosinus ad Sarratantam Episcopum* we get a similar hint:

As man is made of four elements, so also is the stone, and so it arises out of man. Thou art its ore, namely by working. From thee it is extracted, that is, by division. And in thee it remains inseparable.

As we have stated the 'four elements' as used in many of the ancient alchemical texts refers to the grades of the ethereal light. The statement, 'thou art its ore,' and 'from thee it is extracted' means that the stone is made of the substance of one's own body.

The Vajrayana scriptures teach that the illumination of the consciousness is reflected in the *vajra* (indestructible essence) body as a pinpoint of 'clear light,' which, through a secret process, is manifested further as a precipitation (*tiglé*) of one of the chakras. It is then naturally precipitated via the center's corresponding gland into the bloodstream as an amrita or elixir. And when certain internal conditions are met, nature further condenses the tigle into a pearl colored crystal that the Tibetans call *ringsel* and the 'secret bodhichitta.' This precipitation should not be taken symbolically or as a poetic abstraction as it is visible to the inner vision and even, at a certain degree of condensation, to the naked eye. In Tibet the

---

[1] Page 134, footnote 60.

method of condensation was given only to trusted disciples, as it was said to cause harm if one attempted to hasten the process prematurely. The 'secret bodhichitta,' is an external reflection of the internal bodhichitta, the pure selfless motivation to attain enlightenment for the benefit of the world.

The clear light of an illuminated consciousness, the radiant sphere of the purified-regenerated vajra body as a whole, the 'blazing star' of the Rosicrucian and Masonic Mysteries, the *murdhajoytish* of the yogis, the elixir (*amrita*), the red and white drops (*bindus*) of the Buddhist Tantras, the 'crystallized-dew' (*Bedolah*) of the Kabbalah, the Tibetan *ringsel* crystals and the 'gem of many colors' (*sharirum*), are but different degrees of the condensation of the spiritual light stepped down through the highly refined etheric vehicle of the alchemist herself. The condensation of the finest energy is brought about within the finest alchemical laboratory available, the etheric body, though the process has been duplicated on a lower level in the laboratory as well. It is the purest psychic energy that is precipitated, step-by-step, into the Stone of the Wise.

According to Fulcanelli, in his Mystery of the Great Cathedrals, the root of the term crucible is *crux, crucis*, or cross, which is, in one sense, a symbol for the pilgrim himself who has balanced his vertical ascent with the horizontal field of the Great Work.

> *It is in the crucible that the raw material, like Christ himself, suffers the Passion; it is in the crucible that it dies to be resurrected, purified, and spiritualized.*

The etheric body is the hidden crucible, the 'alchemical vase,' the 'glass,' the 'golden bowl,' the mold into which is poured the "Molten Sea" of Hiram Abif, and it may be the 'crystal globe' mentioned by St. Germain in his alchemical masterpiece *The Threefold Sophia*, where he says that it is "the place where the drops drips."[4]

---

[4] See *The Most Holy Trinosophia*. by St. Germain, edited by Manly P. Hall, Philosophical Research Society, 1962, p. LXXI. While the original manuscript was written in French this quote was written in Hebrew, probably to further veil an already very esoteric writing.

In Tibet the crystallization of spiritual energies, generated through wisdom and bliss, is looked for and sometimes found in the ashes after the cremation of highly attained men and women. Lobsang P. Phalungpa describes these crystals in a footnote to his translation of the *Life of Milarepa*:

> *The evolved crystals are generally called 'bodily relics' (kudoong ringsel). They are of tiny pill size, pearl colored, and are found in the ashes of highly attained men and woman. It is widely held that the original evolved crystals multiply if preserved in a proper manner. Hence the 'multiplying bodily relics' — phel doong. Among the types of crystals is that called 'Sharirum', which is said to shine in five hues.[5]*

"The Tibetan ringse[l]," says the author of the Agni Yoga Teaching, "has deep significance being the sediment crystallized by the manifestation of bliss.."[1] Compare the *Sharirum* that 'shines with five hues' with the 'concealed Stone of many colors' found in the *Golden Treatise* of Hermes. In the Buddha's *Sutra of the Great Perfection, (Prajna-Paramita)* it is said that the crystals of the Devas (angel like beings) are far superior to the ones produced by human beings, while the gems of the Tathagatas (Buddhas) are 'the true repositories of the cognition of all knowing.'[2]

In most of the alchemical texts the students are advised to strive for the spiritual light and to pray for wisdom, for it is only through an elevation of consciousness that the descending spiritual Fire is precipitated into the wondrous Pearl of Sophia.

> *Even if one gathers all the power of will, one still cannot evoke the Fire of Space. Those manifestations of the fiery element are not subject to command; they grow naturally from the expansion of consciousness.[3]*

---

[5] *The Life of Milarepa.* Translated by Lobsang P. Lhalungpa, Boulder 1984, p.220.

[1] *Herarchy* # 422. Also see *Heart* # 120

[2] Edward Conze. *The Perfection of Wisdom in Eight Thousands Lines.* Bolinas 1973, pp. 116-118.

[3] *Agni Yoga* 464

Self-mastery, which leads to a mastery of the elements, is a necessary part of the process as it removes one of the primary obstacles to attainment, an undisciplined psychic energy:

To him that overcometh will I give to eat of the hidden manna, and will give him the white stone, and in the stone a new name is written, which no man knoweth saving he that receives it.[1]

'The name, which no man knoweth' is one's inner signature of light. It is said to flash before the mind's eye as geometric symbols and to one's inner ear as a short series of notes. The clairvoyant seer sometimes sees these light signatures as radiant images above the head.[2] Paracelsus, Jacob Boehme, and Rudolf Steiner speak of these essential signatures as representing geometrically and musically one's inner nature.

The illumination of the consciousness finds expression in the light in the head (*murdhajyotishi*).[3] The light is further condensed, via a corresponding gland, as a drop (*bindu*), sometimes called the 'Tears of Isis' or that 'blessed Water which Nature sheds divinely for the world.'[4] This Elixir has also been called White Sulphur, Mother's Milk, and Soma. In the *Book of Light* (*Sefer ha-Zohar*) it was called 'dew' (*bedolah*):

It is written, 'for thy dew is as the dew of light,' which is the shining splendor of the Ancient One... and is seen to have all the colors inside it.... From the external head the dew is distilled... and by that dew, which is in everyone and is discharged from the head, the dead are brought to life for the world to come.[8]

---

[1] *The Book of Revelation:* 2:17

[2] See Theodore Heline's *The Archetype Unveiled: A Study of the Sound Patterns Formed by the Creative Word*. New Age Press 1965. Also see my SENSA The Language of the Sun, page 214

[3] According to the great yogi Gorakhnath this "steady and burning light" is located in what he calls the *gollata-mandapa* center, which is "just above the forehead and in the front-part of the *Sahasrara*." See *The Philosophy of Gorakhnath* by Akshaya Banerjea, page 190.

[4] page 371.

[8] *The Greater Assembly.* # 44, 45, 47, & 51.

Mary Atwood, in her *A Suggestive Inquiry into the Hermetic Mystery*, a chapter on the *Manifestation of the First Matter and its Information by Light* lightly veils many of the secrets of this divine materialization. In many alchemical texts this process is called calcination.

Not by common calcination, which is made by the violence of common fire, but by philosophic calcinations, which is purely natural. [10]

According to the doctrine of Jabir ibn Hayyan (Geber), the great 8th century Arabian alchemists, the calcination process is to be repeated three times; the first produces the Sulphur [soul-fire], the second produces the Elixir, and the third, the Philosopher's Stone. This final Stone says Fulcanelli, "contains all the virtues, qualities and perfections of the Sulphur and the Elixir multiplied in power and in extent."[11]

Thomas Vaughan (Eugenius Philalethes), speaks of the three condensations of the 'universal agent' as gifts of the Virgin:

First, She sheds at Her nipples a thick heavy water, but white as any snow; the philosopher's call it Virgin's Milk. Secondly, She gives him blood from Her heart; it is a quick, heavenly fire; some improperly call it their Sulphur. Thirdly and lastly, She presents him with a secret crystal, of more worth and luster than the white rock and all rosials. [13]

"I reverence Thee Lord [Shiva]," says Abhinavagupta in his esoteric masterwork, *The Tantraloka*, "with the priceless amrita [elixir] of bliss which fills the chalice of my heart." And from the *Rigveda* (VIII, 43, II) we read:

The subtle drop that has entered us, O Pitras,
Is absorbed in our hearts,
That we mortals may become immortal.

The Agni Yoga scriptures state:

---

[10] Mary Atwood. *A Suggestive Inquiry into Hermetic Philosophy*, pages 512-513.

[11] *The Mystery of the Cathedrals.*

[13] Thomas Vaughan. *Coelum Terræ or the Magician's Heavenly Chaos.*

Amrita consists of the precipitates of the finest energies.

The human body is continually renewing itself according to the quality of the psychic energy of its occupant. This process is greatly enhanced by an elevated consciousness, which through the law of attraction, draws subtle energies from above. This is sometimes cryptically referred to as the descent of the Holy Spirit into the chalice or grail. This purifies and refines the consciousness, illuminates and clarifies the mind, and regenerates the body through the precipitation of 'amrita' or 'crystalline dew.' In the *Book of Secrets,* an anonymous, highly esoteric work, which was included in the *Book of Light* collection, we find this veiled statement:

> *The secret of secrets is prepared and arranged in a single skull filled with crystalline dew. The veins of air are purified and sealed. These strands of clean fleece hang down evenly.*

This echo's a similar statement from Solomon's *Song of Songs* 5:2: "My head is filled with dew *(bedolah)* and my locks with the drops of the night." The 'locks' and 'veins of air' refer to the nerve channels *(nadis)* through which the vital 'air' is crystallized into the 'drops in the night,' which descend to the heart. In Medieval Hebrew *bedolah* (dew) also means 'pearl' or 'crystal.' The author of the *Secret of the Golden Flower* writes: "The brilliance of the Light is gradually crystallized."

As the Light-Stone *(abasabindu)* is intensified through the circulation of energies through a triangle of centers, it is then precipitated (materialized) in the head. From there it descends to the heart, drawing up certain energies from below, which are red in color. When the two *tigles* unite we have what Hermes called the marriage of the "crowned King and our Red Daughter." In the Buddhist Tantras this alchemical wedding is symbolically stated to be between the subtle seed (white) and egg (red) from which one's present body was formed.

As the radiant energy emanating from certain radioactive substances can stimulate the activity of other atoms so as to produce nuclear energy, likewise the projection of the radiant energy of the Philosopher's Stone (a crystal of psychic energy) can stimulate the activity of certain nerve centers so as to begin the process of regeneration. In both cases transmutation of the elements takes place. The Teacher has said:

> *Concentrations of the crystals of psychic energy, grow during each heightening of aspiration. Each tension of the power of the spirit multiplies the crystals of psychic energy. Sediments of precipitated crystals, consisting of subtle energies, which have been chemically transformed in the organism, feed those organs that are in special need during the expenditure of energy. Crystals of psychic energy melt down substances harmful for the organism. Through conscious tension one can actually promote this dissolving process, which is of service as a counteracting factor. Conscious sendings of psychic energy to inflected or injured organs can produce a healing effect. Conscious tension of the will causes a spontaneous action of the crystals. Thus thoughts about psychic energy crystals can bring needed assistance for the injuries of internal organs. On the path to the Fiery World it is necessary to realize those fiery batteries, which are contained in man.*[14]

'Conscious tension' and 'tension of the power of spirit,' here means the focusing of psychic energy to a single point of tension, producing at that point a high intensity of energy. Hermes in his *Golden Treatise* speaks of the application of the Stone in a similar way:

> *This, O son, is the concealed Stone of many colors, which is born of one color. Know this and conceal it. By this, the Almighty favoring, the greatest diseases are escaped, and every sorrow, distress, and evil and hurtful things is made to depart. It leads from darkness to light, from this desert wilderness to a secure habitation, and from poverty and straights, to a free and ample fortune.*[15]

Paracelsus writes:

---

14 *The Fiery World Vol. 3 # 218.*
15 *The Golden Treatise*

> *The Philosopher's Stone performs wonders on all diseases. It will drive away any corruption by the method of expulsion and introduce what is good into the human blood by its power of attraction.[16]*

The good that is introduced into the blood is *amrita*.

The Stone can also be used like a magnet to draw out the so-called volatile essence in form that it might, through the application of Vulcan, be reclothed in a new form. This is also alluded to in the *Golden Treatise* of Hermes.

> *Take the flying volatile [the escaping central spark] and drown it flying, seal it within the waters, [an etheric crucible] divide and separate it from its rust [its disintegrating form] which hold it in death. Draw it forth and repel it from itself [from its old form] that it may live and answer thee [remain under thy control], not by flying away into regions above, but by truly forbearing it to fly.*

Throughout many eastern countries the relics of great saints, which often secretly included their bodhichitta crystals, were preserved within stupas, which were specifically created according to the highest principles of sacred geometry for this purpose.1 This was done so that many people could benefit from their radiation by walking around them. These locations literally became magnetized places of spiritual pilgrimage.

---

16   Paraselsus. *A Manual on the Philosopher's Stone.*

1 See my *SENSA, The Language of the Sun.*

According to secret oral tradition within the Ningmapa lineage of Tibet the great Bodhisattva Padmasambhava left behind after his passing many bodhichitta crystals, which as the fulfillment of prophesy was brought from Tibet to 'northwest country' of Oregon to establish there for the future a new spiritual focus.[1]

One of the problems in translating esoteric scriptures is the fact that some words have many levels of meaning depending upon how and even where it is applied. For example the Sanskrit word *bindu* (*thig li* Tibetan) generally means 'drop.' In Buddhist Tantric writings it is often translated as seminal fluid, while technically the levels of meaning run from a point of highly intense subtle energy, through the light drops (*abasabindu*), to those physical and subtle precipitations of the centers (*bindurupabhata*), of which the seminal fluid is but one of many.

Each center has its own precipitation both subtle and dense, which as it crystalized onto the physical plane enters the blood stream via the center's corresponding gland, which is usually in close proximity. Mother's milk, for example, contains a concentration of the mother's heart energy which nourishes the heart and subtle body of the child. The sacral center produces the seed for a new human incarnation. The secret center veiled under the name 'Chalice' produces Soma, a natural elixir. It is through the natural crystallization of the *thig li* that the Philosopher's Stone is precipitated onto the physical plane. For this it is useful to understand the relationship between the etheric nerve centers and the glands, and how the activity of the former produces a corresponding activity in the latter. The esoteric books, written by Master D.K. and published under the name of his student Alice Bailey, are some of the best and most reliable sources for information on the etheric nerve centers. These books are veiled primarily through an over abundance of information scattered over many volumes.

The reason for the sexual symbolism often found in some very reliable esoteric teachings is that the process of the conception, growth, and birth of a child in the womb of the mother corresponds closely to the conception, growth, and birth of the luminous body of the initiates. As this

---

[1] Tashi Choling

process is one of the secrets of initiation, one of the ways in which it can be accurately described, without revealing dangerous secrets to the uninitiated, is through direct analogy. Tibetan deities, for example, that show the union of male and female figures (*yab yum*), are symbolic of the realization of spiritual union on higher levels.

Lobsang P. Lhalungpa, in his translation of the *Madhmudra: The Quintessence of Mind and Meditation,* comments on the practice of using a sex partner in tantra exercises:

> *In Tibet it was generally discouraged and in any case no celibate monk or lama was allowed to practice it. Many great teachers opposed it on the grounds that it [the teachings on the subject] could not be interpreted literally, since the higher tantric texts are purposely written in a peculiar language that must be deciphered through the six modes and four methods. The true meaning of the concept appertains to the integration of the higher psychophysical elements, energies and creative forces inside and around an individual human body.[17]*

Natural precipitations of subtle energy within the vegetable and animal kingdoms that are useful in healing and the increase of vitality include the resins of cedar, pine, eucalyptus, and acacia trees, raw milk and honey, and musk. Musk, which is one of the secret ingredients of a Tibetan amrita, is also mentioned in the Agni Yoga Teaching as being useful.

The spiritual Hierarchy, the great Sangha of Bodhisattvas, Masters of Wisdom, call them what you will, have taught that the missing keys and higher correspondence of this most sacred science are to be supplied orally by an initiate of the Brotherhood. The saying is true; "When the student is ready the master will appear!"

Mary Atwood, in her *A Suggestive Inquiry into the Hermetic Mystery,* writes:

> *Alchemy, is a universal art of vital chemistry, which opens the elementary germ into new life and consciousness. It manifests as a*

---

[17] p. 438, note # 9

concrete essence of Light, which essence is the true form or idea of gold. This process takes place in and through the human body in the blood, changing the relation of its components parts or principles, and reversing the circulatory order, so that, the sensible medium becomes occult, the inner source of its vitality is awakened and the consciousness at the same time being centrally drawn, comes to know and feel itself in its own true Source, which is the Universal Center and source of all things.

Jacob Boehme states:

If we consider now the springing up of the Life and in what Place of the body where the Life is generated, then we shall rightly find the Whole Ground of Man, for there is nothing so secret in Man that it may not be found. For we must say, that the Heart is the place where the New Life is generated and the Life again penetrates the Heart.20

The esoteric scriptures tell us that it is only through the union of wisdom and active compassion that the red and white bindus are united at the heart center and not through visualization alone. Only when the higher centers are active as a result of corresponding levels of consciousness and they become balanced and tempered in the fire of the heart are the bodhichitta crystals created.

The mystery of the heart essence of the mystical alchemist is profound. The fire of the heart generates wisdom and active compassion, transmuting the illusion of separation into the realization of essential unity or 'non-duality' as it is sometimes called. The fire of the heart refines and expands the consciousness, producing clear vision. On the etheric plane it transmutes the energies of the lower centers into their higher counterparts. All true progress on the path that is instep with the evolution of consciousness is dependent upon the heart essence, the alchemical fire.

In the *Life of Apolionius* by Philostratus we find this statement concerning the Light and the Stone:

---

[20] *The Three Principles of Divine Essence.*

It is the wise only, who by means of certain verbal formula and rites, can attain the Pentarba. That is the name of the Stone, which at night has the appearance of fire, being flaming and sparkling, while in the day it dazzles by its brightness. This light is a subtle matter of admirable virtue, for it attracts all that is near to it in likeness.

Eliphas Levi, comments on this passage, says that the Philosopher's Stone is formed of the astral light condensed and fixed about a center.[3] Peter Davidson writes of this subtle light in his little known classic work on the essence of the Zohar called *The Book of Light and Life.*

This Light, Kabalistically speaking, is that unique substance, mediator of movement, unfading and eternal, which engenders every thing and to which every thing returns. . . . It is at the same time in the phenomenal world the sperm of matter and the matrix of forms, however contradictory this may appear at first sight. . . . It is that universal, imponderable fluid whose four sensible manifestations are termed Heat, Light, Electricity and Magnetism. It is the Akasha of the Hindus, the Aour of the Hebrews, the Astral Light of Martin and Levi, the Sidereal Light of Paracelsus. . . . In simpler language, it is the Ruach Elohim of Moses, the Divine Ether of the Greeks, the Mens or Spiritus of the Romans. . .

These names pertain to different grades of the one universal subtle-energy, animating and vitalizing all aspects of manifested universe. Blavatsky called this Fire the "Matrix of the Universe, the Mysterium Magicum from which all that exists is born by separation."

The Paracelsus, Jacob Boehme, and the Rosicrucian Brotherhood, secretly identified the Philosopher's Stone with the perfected indestructible diamond body of light as a whole. This does not contradict what we have stated above, as the greater includes the lesser and together forms a single principle of great radiance and power. Jacob Boehme gives this moderately veiled hint:

---

[3] Levi, Eliphas. A History of Magic. N.Y. 1971, p. 164.

The noble Philosopher's Stone is as easy to find as any other stone. It may adorn the outer life with gold, silver and precious stones, all to our joy and to God's deeds of wonder. We do not need the clothing of beasts for we can go naked, clothed in a heavenly tincture.[1]

There are, of coarse, many grades and qualities to these 'evolved crystals,' from the secret bodhichitta of the an Arhat, all the way to those Great Stones of Power that are the creative focus for a complete hierarchy of lives, deva or human. Very little is known of these Stones beyond what has been passed down to us through myths and legends.[2] These great Stones include:

1. The Vajra Scepter of Indra, which was formed, it is said, of the evolved crystal of the ancient Rishi Dadhica.

2. The Trisula, or trident of Shiva, which is said to have been condensed (or distilled) eight times from a ray of the purest sunlight.

3. The Pearl of Sophia, which according to Jacob Boehme is the great Stone of power of one of the Angelic Hierarchies. He once asked the Goddess Sophia for a glimpse of this Stone but She refused.

4. The Kustibha or Stone of Vishnu, which was given, we are told, to Krishna.

5. The Rod of Initiation, which is welded by the Hierophant during initiation into the first two degrees of the Mysteries. According to Clemens Alexandrinu it is the Lord Himself [Christ] that confers initiation. "Blessed now that I have been initiated. It is the Lord himself who is the Hierophant." This in confirmed by D. K. who says that the Christ is the initiator of the first two initiations. The Stone of Vishnu and the Rod of Initiation may be one and the same.

6. The Flaming Diamond, a Vajra of Great Power, which according of Master D.K., is only welded by the King of Shamballa, Lord of the

---

[1] *The Threefold Life of Man.*

[2] Many world-class myths and legends have their origin in the Mysteries. Great truths were often given to public in the form of symbolic stories as a way of preserving, for those with ears to here, important information concerning the spiritual evolution of the world.

World, the Ancient of Days, during initiation into the 'Greater Mysteries.' When the Stone of Initiation, comes in contact with certain centers of the etheric body, according to the need and level of the initiate concerned, they are transmuted into a higher dimensional frequency.

Master D.K. has stated that initiation takes place upon the mental plane, though the etheric body, but not the physical body, is also involved in the process. Several initiate writers, including Rudolf Steiner and H.P. Blavatsky, confirm this. St. Paul, St. John, Dionysius of Areopagite, Ibn 'Arabi, and Proclus have hinted that initiation takes place outside of the body. Blavatsky states that during initiation into the Mysteries the physical body of the candidate, simulating death, was often placed in a casket while the soul consciousness ascended to the spiritual worlds for three days (some say three and a half days) in a vesture of light to receive initiation. Rudolf Steiner, a seer of remarkable abilities, gives us a rare glimpse concerning the beginning and end of a the initiation process, though on the initiation itself he remains silent:

Within the Mysteries in those ancient times every human being who was to receive initiation was led into a special chamber. The walls were black, the whole space was dark and gloomy, empty save for a coffin, or something not unlike a coffin. Beside the coffin those who accompanied the candidate for Initiation broke forth into songs of mourning, songs of death. The candidate was treated like one who is about to die. He was given to understand that when he was now laid in the coffin, he would have to undergo what the human being undergoes in the first three days after death. On the third day there appeared at a certain place, within sight of the one who lay in the coffin, a twig or a branch to represent the thriving life of spring. And now the songs of mourning were transferred into hymns of joy and praise. With a transformed consciousness, the man arose out of his grave. A new language, a new writing, was communicated to him; it was the language and writing of spiritual Beings. Henceforth he was allowed to see the world — for now indeed he could *see it — from the standpoint of the Spirit.*

In ancient times the lesser initiations took place, we are told, in certain secret temples, physical outposts of the Hierarchy. As the downward involutionary arch began to dominate during the Kali Yuga there was a gradual decline of these outer Mystery centers. Eventually they disappeared completely from public view. It should be emphasized however that the hidden Brotherhood and the Mysteries continue to this day and initiation still takes place when the candidate is ready, though in complete secrecy.

There are several prophecies concerning the restoration of the Mysteries, the science of Initiation, and the reappearance of the Brotherhood on earth. According to Master D.K. this will begin to take place after the year 2025.

Fragments of the outer ritual of the lesser initiations have been preserved in the Eucharist of the Catholic Church, Tibetan empowerments, and in some of the rituals of the Masonic Lodges. And while these are undoubtedly but symbolic fragments from the original it would make an interesting and useful study to compare the initiation rituals of these three very different cultures. The Essenes enacted a symbolic form of initiation in the 'baptism' ritual made famous through John the Baptist. Some of the rituals now used in the Catholic Mass were taken directly from those writings of Dionysius the Areopagite symbolically depicting the initiation process.[1] As Rudolf Steiner points out, Dionysius gave a fairly accurate description of some of the secret teachings that were taught in St. Paul's school in Athens.

In many of the alchemical texts the Philosopher's Stone is said to cure all diseases, regenerate the body even to the point of physical immortality. Rudolf Steiner said, "For those who understand how to use the Philosopher's Stone, death occurs in appearance only."

In Percival by …….. we are told that the Stone and the Holy Grail are on and the same. In one sense this is true, but only at the highest level of completion. The Holy Grail of the medieval romances not only represents the

---

[1] Dionysius the Areopagite, *Divine Names & The Celestial Hierarchies,* translated by the editors of The Shrine of Wisdom.

crucible in which the Philosopher's Stone is forged, it provides the radiant substance needed for its manifestation.

.

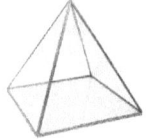

Exodus

At midnight I saw a sun shining with a splendid light.
Apuleius

Pass on, O pilgrim, with steady perseverance. No candle is there nor earth lamp fed with oil. Ever the radiance groweth till the path ends with a blaze of glory, and the wanderer through the night becommeth the child of the sun, and entereth within the portals of that radiant orb.   An Ancient Scripture

Let him discern the jewel set in the forehead of the serpent whose tail he holds, and by its radiance traverse the miry halls of maya.   The Old Commentary

Mary Atwood, in her *A Suggestive Inquiry into the Hermetic Mystery*, defines the goal of Hermetic Science as the conscious development of the causal principle in the human kingdom.

Modern science, with all its abundance of facts—dead, living, and traditional—has not advanced one step in Causal Science. Effects indeed are found to indicate their causes and so we infer many things and progress

externally: but no one particular of nature is more intrinsically understood.
And after a lapse of many centuries of persevering toil and expectation—still,
in the same maze of external nature, dissatisfied and unhappy, amidst the
passing images of his own outward creation; without a ray of the First Light to
guide him into the inner courts of a more certain and sublime experience.

To discover the causal principle in man we must first look to the
divine impulse, hidden within him, to return to the source and essence of
his being. It is by consciously uniting with this original impulse that the
spiritual light is awakened. It is through the assimilation of this spiritual
light that the human organism is regenerated and eventually transformed
into a radiant body of light. This takes place naturally when the
consciousness has been awakened, mastered, refined, and eventually
transformed. It is transformed completely when it can leave behind its
habitual attachment to and identification with the world of the senses, pass
through what has been called the Gate of Brahma, (*Brahmarandhara*), and
sour to the heights of clear perception and being. In this form of alchemy
the Heavenly Flyer, or escaping volatile essence, is the consciousness
principle, which when freed from the confines of its three fold lower
nature (i.e. physical, emotional, and conceptual reasoning mind) acts as a
bridge, uniting the descending spiritual current with the mind and vital
body, transforming these two bodies into a single dynamo of light and
power.

At a certain stage in this transformation process there is a peculiar
condition that has been described by some mystics as passing through a
long dark tunnel of extreme isolation and emerging out into spiritual unity
and light. St. John of the Cross spoke of this transition stage as passing
through the 'dark night of the soul,' where due to an ever increasing sense
of divinity the pilgrim leaves behind his identification with the body to
merge with the divine. It is called a 'dark night,' because at this point one
experiences utter isolation. The world of the senses has been temporarily
left behind and the full emergence into the higher worlds still lies ahead.
The psychological keynote of this transitional period, this exodus from all
that is familiar, is one of isolation and obscurity. St. John of the Cross says:

Our Lord leads souls into the dark night in order to bring them through it to divine union. . . obscurity in regards all that the eye sees, the ear hears, the imagination represents and the heart perceives.[1]

The Sufis call this dark night experience *al-fatra* or 'the divine silence.' The great Sufi saint, Ibn 'Arabi writes of his painful experience with *fatra* as a perilous test. *Fatra* is also know in the Sufi community as 'abandonment' and 'crossing the desert.'[1] According to Master D. K. This 'occult blindness' takes place with graduated degrees of severity during the first four initiations.[2] In some of the Masonic rituals as well as in many of the Tibetan empowerments the candidates for initiation wear a symbolic blindfold, symbolic of the mysterious blindness.

The Bodhisattva Avalokiteshvara, in the *Surangama Sutra,* described his withdraw from the world of the senses during meditation:

I was at first in a state of isolation, in which I could feel neither stillness nor movement of the phenomenal world. Gradually, even the sense of hearing itself disappeared. This was followed by a sense of emptiness in which I did not have any sensations at all. When the sense of emptiness completed itself, the emptiness itself was also gone. In this state of no-birth and no-death, nirvana was realized.

Thomas Vaughn called this exodus of the consciousness from the world of the senses as the 'darkest night' and the 'horrible emptiness.' Rudolf Steiner describes this state by saying that it is the "loneliness of the soul raised to the supreme degree."[3] Dr. R. P. Kaushik in his book *Organic Alchemy* called it the 'spontaneous silence.'

If you can stay in this dark tunnel or dark night then you will find a wonderful thing happening, that this silence or void is transformed, the human mind is no longer a human mind in an ordinary sense. It is now one single divine energy. Once this communion with the divine takes place,

[1] St. John of the Cross. *The Ascent of Mt. Carmel.*

[1] See Claude Addas' *Quest for the Red Sulphur, page 43.*

[2] See Alive Bailey's *The Rays and the Initiations,* pages 197-200.

[3] *Initiation, Eternity and the Passing Moment,* page 85.

your brain cells undergo a radical transformation. Once this transformation begins in your brain cells it is reflected in your body.[2]

The avenue through which the exodus of consciousness takes place is what the Bailey Books call the Antahkarana or Rainbow Bridge, connecting the mental body with our innermost threefold essential nature, also called the Spiritual Triad. The portal through which one must pass to enter the higher worlds, temporally leaving behind the sense world, is the twelve-petalled brahmarandhara center at the top of the head. In alchemical literature this doorway has been given many names—the 'gate of heaven,' the 'opening of the mysterious female,' and the 'hole of Brahma.' This center, like its lower counterpart, the heart center, is a twelve petalled lotus. Master D.K. calls it the 'the heart in the head.' The great yogi Gorakhnath calls it the Nirvana center. The consciousness principle anchored in the body cannot pass through this gate, we are told, until one's vibrational frequency matches, or is in harmony with the vibrational intensity of this center.

When the consciousness has been refined and purified in what has been called the 'fire of the heart' the yogi can exodus through this doorway, and two more (one for each of the three bodies through which one must pass) following the guiding light that the *Old Commentary* calls 'the light which guides through the triple caves of darkness.' St. Germain, in his highly veiled manuscript, *The Divine Three Fold Sophia,* called this light the 'Flaming Star.'[1] It is first seen with the mind's eye as a light in the head (*murdha-jotish*). D.K. gives a description of this light in his *A Treatise on White Magic:*

> *Frequently students speak of a diffused light or glow, this is the light of the physical plane atoms of which the brain is composed; later they speak of seeing what appears to be like a sun in the head. This is the contacting of the etheric light, plus the physical atomic light. Later they become aware of an intensely bright electric light; this is the soul light, plus the etheric and the*

---

2 R.P. Kaushik. *Organic Alchemy*, page 2.

1 See page 127 below.

atomic. When this is seen, they frequently become aware of a dark centre within the radiant sun. This is the entrance to the Path disclosed by the 'shining of the light upon the door.'[3]

Sailendra Das Gupts, author of the book *Kriya Yoga*, has this to say concerning the light in the head:

[It] appears as a bright sphere of white light with a deep blue central spot. The white aura is considered as Radha by Kriya Yogis and the deep blue, almost black, central spot is Shri Krishna, the reflection of the Kutastha Chitanya.[4]

The name, Kutastha Chitanya, means the 'one at the summit,' Shri Krishna here represents the soul and Radha is the soul's radiant material expression. The white light is the *materia lucida*, the radiant light of etheric matter itself, while the dark blue (indigo) center is a reflection of the light of the soul. The indigo light is the entrance to the path to the higher worlds. D.K. continues:

At the very center of the light [in the head] is a center or point of dark indigo blue — midnight blue. Note the significance of this in view of what I have been saying anent the 'dark night,' the midnight hour, the zero hour in the life of the soul. That center is in reality an opening, a door leading somewhere, a way of escape, a place through which the soul imprisoned in the body can emerge and pass into higher states of consciousness, untrammeled by form limitations, it has been called the 'funnel or channel for the sound'; it has been named 'the trumpet through which the escaping A. U. M. can pass.'[5]

In the sacred scriptures of ancient India it is said that the *Jivatma* or incarnating spirit, eventually escapes the prison house of the body through the Brahmarandhara center. The four angels with their flaming swords,

---

[3] Page. 107

[4] Page 144

[5] *The Rays and the Initiations.*

who guard the entrance to Eden (a symbol for the etheric plane) from premature entrance, are the *Agnishvattas* or Solar Angels. They allow the righteous exodus from the physical body during enlightenment only when the vibrational rate of that center matches or synchronizes with a certain exalted level of consciousness.

> *They [the solar angels] represent a peculiar type of electrical force. Their work is to blend and fuse, and above all they are the 'transmuting fires' of the system, and are those agents who pass the life of God through their bodies of flame as it descends from the higher into the lower and again as it ascends from the lower into the higher.[6]*

Thomas Vaughan gives a veiled description of the light in the head in his esoteric work *Lumen De Lumine*, or *New Magical Light*. His method of veiling here is to disguise his statements with a liberal sprinkling of unnecessary words. The hidden meaning begins to emerge when these distracting words are removed.

> *And I saw a weak white light. . . . Towards the center it was of a purple color, like a Elysian sunshine, but in the dilation of the circumference, milky white. . . . Out of the very center did unfold a certain flowery light. . . . Very bright it was, sparkling and twinkling like a day-star. . . . I conceived it to be the Temple of Nature.*

As the daystar, the sun, it continues to shine in the minds eye. Thomas Vaughan goes on to say that the Romans called this light the Sol Mortuorum, a term which has also been used to describe the light at the end of tunnel seen in the near death experience. For a human being it is through this tunnel of light that righteous exodus occurs. Through this light, Vaughan tells us, that he was able to make contact with Thalia, the Goddess of Nature, who revealed to him many of nature's secrets. "Through one-pointed concentration upon the light in the head (mudra-

---

6 *A Treatise on Cosmic Fire.* p. 698.

jyotisi)" says Patanjali in his Yoga Sutras, "a vision of the perfected Ones can be attained."[7]

Yogananda, who received teachings on this science from the immortal Master known to him as Babaji, called the dark pathway through the *mudrajyotis* (light in the head), the 'dark blue tunnel,' 'the cave of silence,' and the 'spiritual eye.' When the spiritual vision becomes clear, he says, the light at the end of the tunnel takes the form of a five-pointed star ☆. This gives new meaning to the cryptic statement found in the Masonic *Ritual of the Degree of the Kabalistic and Hermetic Rose:*

> *The birth of the Sun [in the head] is always announced by its Star, represented by the Blazing Star [☆], which you will know by its fiery color and is followed by the silvery luster of the moon.*

This is confirmed by Master D.K.:

> *He becomes aware of growing point of light which, from a pin-point of intensest brilliance develops before him into a five pointed star.[8]*

Yogananda, in one of his private lessons given through the Self-Realization Fellowship, gives the following description of this triple path (i.e. the light in the head, the dark blue tunnel, and the light at the end of the tunnel), calling it a Spiritual Eye:

> 1. A little star in the center corresponding to the pupil of the eye. This five-pointed star is the door to infinity.
> 2. A dark blue circle around the star, corresponding to the iris of the physical eye.
> 3. A golden white halo around the blue light corresponds to the white of the physical eye.[9]

Yogananda continues:

----

[7] 3: 32
[8] *The Rays and the Initiations,* p. 176.
[9] # 153

[The spiritual eye is entered by] reversing the outward flow of the life force through the senses. [Then the yogi sees] a white light increasing like an aurora in a spiritual eye — with closed or open eyes. Then, when the breath disappears and the life force movement retires from the nerves, eyes and the nuclei of the cells, the current becomes deeper and becomes projected into the infinite, creating a dark blue tunnel into the center of the spiritual eye. This current spreads into the bottomless heart of Infinity, revealing an endless tunnel of dim light through which the soul must pass.

Master D.K. veils the process using symbolic images:

Enter the cave and find your own, walk in the dark and carry a lighted lamp. The cave is dark and lonely. . . . The cave is long and narrow. . . . Far off, dim and most vaguely seen appears an oval opening, its color blue. Stretched athwart this space of blue, a rosy cross is seen, and at the center of the cross where the four arms meet, a rose. Upon the upper limb a vibrant diamond shines, within a star five-pointed. The living soul drives forward toward the cross. . . [and] out into radiant life and light![10]

The Blazing Star, the Flaming Diamond, and the Rose and Cross, all significant symbols of ancient Mysteries, appear to the awakened vision as geometric signposts on the Path of Light, woven from the *prima materia* of one's own energy body, thus giving meaning to the statement that 'one must become the Path itself.'

Enlightenment, the illumination of the mind, is not a poetic or psychological abstraction. Subtle light or luminous energy/substance (*materia lucida*), descending from above, illuminating the inner vision of the spiritual eye in the same way that physical light illuminates the field of vision for the physical eyes. D.K. says:

The third eye manifests as a result of the vibratory interaction between the forces of the soul, working through the pineal gland, and the forces of the

---

[10] Bailey. Discipleship in the New Age. Vol 1, pp. 675-676.

personality working through the pituitary body. These negative and positive forces interact, and when potent enough produce the light in the head. Just as the physical eye came into being in response to the light of the sun so the spiritual eye came into being in response to the light of the spiritual sun.[11]

A similar idea can be found in the *Secret of the Golden Flower*:

In the midst of primal becoming,
The radiance of the light is the determining thing.
In the physical world it is the sun,
In man, the eye.

To many cultures the sun was thought to be an eye through which the Gods looks out upon the worlds. In Vedic mythology *Surya*, the being whose body is the sun, is known as *Loka Chakshuh*, the Eye of the World. To the Persians the sun was the eye of Ormuzd. To the Egyptians it was the right eye of Demiurge, and in the so-called *Book of the Dead* the sun was often represented as an eye. To the Greeks it was the eye of Zeus. The early Teutons regarded it as the eye of Oden. Jacob Boehme called the sun the 'All-seeing-eye.'

According to the teachings of the great yogi Gorakhnath, all the chakras at a certain stage in their unfoldment produce a subtle light. He locates the *murdha-jyotish* (light in the head) at the center between the two eyes where it takes the form of a steady burning lamplight the size of the thumb. This he calls *Jananetra*, the eye of wisdom. He goes on to say that this inner light illumines the consciousness of the yogi whose attention is concentrated upon it.[12] "The hidden light," says the *Zohar*, "is the light of the eye. . . . With it the holy one can see from one end of the universe to the other." Master D.K. said:

---

[11] *A Treatise on White Magic.* p.213.

[12] Alshaya K, Banerjea. *The Philosophy of Gorakhnath.* p. 179

The mystery of the eye, and its relation to light (esoterically understood) is very great, and as yet no student, no matter how diligent, knows anything about it.[13]

In the language of the Hermetic Mysteries 'Light' is often used to mean the all pervading Primordial Energy, which like the sun shins it energy upon us from above. The 'eye' was sometimes used to veil a door through with the consciousness could enter to perceive the higher world. Valentin Tomberg in his work on the *Apocalypse,* says that this open door ensures "unhindered intercourse with the spiritual world."

It appears to the spiritual eye as a special formation of the etheric head organism. The appearance is such that a 'radiant crown' is seen upon the head — a crown which is the expression of those ascending and descending spiritual currents, whose presence reveals the faculty of the 'open door.'[15]

According to the *Book of the Yellow Castle*, an ancient alchemical text of early Taoism, the light or splendor is found "in the field of the square inch of the house of the square foot." The 'square inch' lies between the eyebrows while the 'house of the square foot' is the head.

In the middle of the square inch dwells the splendor. Confucius called it the center of emptiness; the Buddhist, the terrace of life; the Taoists, the ancestral land, the yellow castle or the dark pass. . . .If then the true seed is born, and the right method applied in order to melt and mix it, and in that way to create the Elixir of Life, then one goes through the pass.[17]

The Chinese alchemist Liu I-ming defines the 'gate of heaven' as the "center at the top of the head from which the spirit is projected into enlightenment." It has also been called the 'true opening of the mysterious female.'

---

[13] Bailey. *Discipleship in the New Age.* Vol. 2, p. 348.

[15] p.65

[17] *The Secret of the Golden Flower.* N.Y. 1935, Wilhelm translation. pp.24 & 26.

If students want to practice the great Tao and to comprehend the essence of life, they should find the opening of the mysterious female which is the opening of the mysterious pass.[18]

Master D.K. writes:

As evolution proceeds, these dim points of 'dark light' intensify their glow; the light within the head flickers at intervals during the life of the average man, and becomes a shining light as he enters upon the path of discipleship. When he becomes an initiate, the light of the atoms is so bright, and the light in the head so intense (with a paralleling stimulation of the centres of force in the body), that the light body appears. Eventually this body of light becomes externalized and of greater prominence than the dense tangible physical body. This is the body of light in which the true Son of God consciously dwell.

---

[18] Chang Po-tuan. *The Inner Teachings of Taoism*. Boston 1986

The Body of Light

To him that overcometh I will give to eat of the hidden Manna, I will give him the White Stone. . . I will give the Morning Star. To him that overcometh shall be clothed in a White Raiment.   The Book of Revelation

And thou will come ready to receive thy vestment. For, wherefore the power and wherefore the sacrifice if there is no joy? And where is compassion, and where is the love of creation, if thy shoulders are not bedecked with the Raiment of the Mother of the world?   Leaves of Morya's Garden

Sickness, old age, and death does not touch one who has attained the body made from the fire of yoga.
          The Shetashvatara Upanishad

ulcanelli, the great French alchemists and author of *The Mystery of the Cathedrales*, when asked about making gold, answered: "That is only one aspect of it, a special case. The vital thing is not the transmutation of metals but the worker himself." Basil Valentine, one of the greatest of the seventeenth century alchemists, clearly indicates that the purpose behind the practice of alchemy is "…that his Body may be transmuted into a Holy Temple of God…"[1]

Initiates of the Mysteries were often called Temple Builders. This title can be understood in three ways—physically, spiritually, and secret. The initiate builders created cathedrals, temples, and stupas in the attempt to recreate on the physical plane a geometric likeness of divine principles.[2] The idea being that due to their geometric shapes those who entered these temples partook, even if unconsciously, of portion of the principles thus depicted. The study of the psychological and spiritual influence of geometric shapes will someday become a major field of study. The success of this work can be measured by its beauty; in fact the success of the Great Work on all levels can be measured by the resultant beauty. The greater the beauty the greater will be the truth being represented.

The spiritual Temple Builders worked in to create the inner Temple of the Soul, which the Theosophists call the Causal Body and the Cabalists symbolize by the Temple of Jerusalem. It is built as the manifestation of attained spiritual qualities takes effect in the soul.

The secret temple pertains to the human equivalent to the Hiranyagarbha, the Golden Egg from which the worlds were created or that which Blavatsky and Master D.K. have called the Auric Egg,[3] from which manifested a beautiful Rainbow Body of Light. James Pryse, a student of H.P. Blavatsky, writes in his illuminating work *A New Presentation of the Prometheus Bound of Aischylos*:

> *The immortal Self of man, his true 'Life,' is a Monad, which for its initial manifestation is ensphered in Light; within this sphere, and derived therefrom, is the immortal spiritual body, referred to in Greek mysticism as the luciform vesture, augoeides chiton.*[4]

And in his *Apocalypse Unsealed* Pryse writes more on this subject:

---

[1] *Triumphant Chariot of Antimony*, London 1678, page 2.

[2] See Adrian Snodgrass, *The Symbolism of the Stupa*.

[3] See Blavatsky, *The Esoteric Writings of H.P. Blavatsky*.

[4] Page 86.

The esotericist understands that true self-knowledge can be attained only through self-development in the highest sense of the term, a development which begins with introspection and the awakening of creative and regenerative forces which now slumber in man's inner protoplasmic nature, like the vivific potency in the ovum, and which when roused into activity transform him ultimately into a divine being embodied in a deathless ethereal form of ineffable beauty. This process of transcendental self-conquest, the giving birth to oneself as a spiritual being, evolving from the concealed essence of one's own embryonic nature a self-luminous immortal body.[1]

The term 'ovum' here points to its higher correspondence, the luminous auric egg which surrounds and gives life to the complete organism, spiritual and physical. 'The self-luminous immortal body,' arises, we are told here, by a process of 'transcendental self-conquest,' and through 'the creative and regenerative forces' of the auric envelope. The manifestation of the luminous body is woven into form, says Pryse, through the action of psychic energy:

It is this force which, in telestic work, or cycle of initiation, weaves from the primal substance of the auric ovum, upon the ideal form of archetype it contains, and conforming thereto, the immortal Augoeides, or solar body (soma heliakon), so called because in its visible appearance it is self-luminous like the sun, and has a golden radiance.[2]

H.P. Blavatsky, in her secret instructions to the Esoteric Section of the Theosophical Society,[3] writes:

The 'Luminous Egg' (Hiranyagarbha) is the invisible magnetic sphere in which every man is enveloped. It is a direct emanation from: A) The Atmic Ray... and B) Buddhi-Manas. The seventh aspect of this Aura is the facility of assuming the form of its body and becoming the radiant and luminous Augoeides. It is this, strictly speaking, which at times becomes the form called Mayavi Rupa. It is also the material from which the Adept

---

[1] Pages 8 & 9.

[2] *Apocalypse Unsealed* page 12.

[3] Reprinted in the so-called third volume of the Secret Doctrine.

forms his astral (etheric) bodies, from the Augoeides and Mayavi Rupa downwards.1

Thus the mysterious 'Luminous Egg' is the direct emanation of the spiritual triad, *Atma, Buddhi,* and *Manas,* the three highest principles of a human being. According to the Greek Mysteries the Augoeides (*Αυγοειδές*) refers to the luminous body in which a perfected human being, dwells. The '*mayavirupa*' is a self-created human etheric-physical body which the adept creates as needed in the Great Work. Brother D.K. in his *The Rays and the Initiations,* 'a book written primarily for initiates,' says that:

> *The work of the initiate is to aid in the construction of the planetary body of light-substance which will finally reveal the nature of Deity and the glory of the Lord. It is the planetary correspondence to the light-body through which Christ and all the Sons of God that have reached perfection finally manifest. It is a vehicle created by the energy of Will. It expresses itself exoterically by the projection of this will energy, via the central point in each of the seven charkas or lotuses.²*

It we examine this passage carefully we learn that one of the goals of both world and individual evolution, is the spiritualization of the energy/substance of the physical plane through the externalization of a body of light and fire.

The manifestation of the light body is the result of illumination, which is the inflow and absorption of Light from above. Illumination descends from above; it is not generated from below. All we can do as personalities is to strive to unify with the divine and to remove the obstacles to the resultant descent of spiritual energies. The obstructions, which, for the most part, we have created ourselves, individually and collectively, are removed through purification and self mastery of the consciousness and its three vehicles of expression, the etheric body, the feeling body, and the mental body. It is a part of the great Law of

---

1 As quoted in *The Key to the Universe* by Harriette Curtiss, page 51. Also see *The Esoteric Writings of Blavatsky,* pages 356.

2 Page 184

Equilibrium that for every upward striving there is an equal downward flow of the spiritual Light (Shakti-Energy). The descent of the Light is ruled by the law of attraction. Like attracts like. Whatever we think about, what ever we feel strongly about, is reflected in kind in three worlds. This karmic law forms the basis of the health or ill-health of body. The closer that our thoughts and feelings harmonize with the higher frequencies the greater will be the manifestation of those spiritual energies into our lives and vehicles.

In Mary Atwood's *The Hermetic Mystery,* we find the following veiled statement. I have taken the liberty of filling in and clarifying the missing words in brackets, a process that is often necessary when deciphering genuine esoteric works.

> *Let us now conceive the Vital Essence [of the etheric body] theurgically purified [through communion with the Gods] and freed of all foreign attractions, revolving about its centre and having power, active and passive, in hypostatic union [of the primary energy (active) and the etheric body as a whole (passive)] always about to generate the infinite fullness which it contains and draws [down from above] as even now we approach [in our studies], carrying along with us the body of the Sphinx [a composite of the three vehicles of the personality], subdued and contrite [through self-mastery], to the gate of the first Adytum [the Holy of Holies] where we would contemplate awhile, in the vestibule [of that gateway to initiation] admiring the Tears of Isis [the descending drops of amrita] even that blessed Water which Nature sheds divinely to the world.*

'The blessed Water which Nature sheds divinely to the world' is the descending spiritual Light, which illuminates the mind, precipitates the amrita and pentarba, and eventually manifests the immortal body of fire. Iamblichus (d. AD 330), in his esoteric treatise *On the Mysteries*, says that theurgy is the invocation of, and union with, the Gods, which thereby attracts "the divine fire, which shines universally on its own initiative, self-summoned and self-energized."

The principle thing in invoking the Spirit, that is seen coming down and entering into an individual, is its quality and influence. The fire is sometimes seen by the recipient before receiving it. It is sometime seen by others during its descent.

"And there appeared to them tongues of fire which descended upon them. And they were filled with the Holy Spirit."[1]

The descent of the spiritual Light (Holy Spirit, Shakti, Primary Energy, or whatever you wish to call it) regenerating and illuminating the spirit, mind, and body. It is a fundamental law of Nature that whatever takes place on the plane of mind will manifest in the etheric body and by reflex the dense physical body as well. It is this law that gives creative thinking its power to manifest and why the mastery and utilization of psychic energy is so vital to our present stage in evolution. It is also what gives the alchemist the power to manifest the abstracted essence into a new form. It is this principle law that explains some what the activity of Karma. Thought and emotional harmonies or imbalances materialize corresponding energy/substance in the etheric body, which remains, sometimes for lifetimes, until it manifests as physical activity or events in the life of their creator.

The mystery of the descent, absorption, and radiation of the spiritual Light by the initiate approaching the inner Adytum, the Holy of Holies, is one of the central themes of the ancient Mysteries. It has been veiled behind such terms as Initiation, Fiery Baptism, the descent of the Holy Spirit, and the Return of the Mother. In the Eleusinian Mysteries the baptism ceremony symbolically depicted the descent of spiritual energies to the candidate for initiation. James Pryse, in his illuminating work concerning the candidate's approach to the Greater Mysteries, *The Adorers of Dionysos,* writes:

In the Eleusinian ceremonial the candidates of the Lesser Mysteries were baptized in the river Ilissos by Hydranos, the Water-initiator, who thus personified Zeus, who is represented in the zodiac as the Water-pourer,

---

[1] Acts 2 1-13

Aquarius (Hydrochoos). But the Son of Zeus [Dionysos] who is mightier than his father, baptizes in the Great Breath and in Fire; and the Greater Mysteries were those of Dionysos and Demeter.... The psychic forces have been likened to water, and the higher energies to fire. The purification by water must precede the baptism of fire, the vital electricity which is emblematized by the thyrus of Dionysos, the God of Seership.

John the Baptist said:

I baptize you with water for repentance. But after me comes one who is more powerful than I, whose sandals I am not worthy to carry. He will baptize you with the Fire of the Holy Breath.

The Hebrew term *rauch,* which basically means breath, is usually translated as spirit. To be baptized by the Holy Breath means to receive the outflowing the Breath of God. When the Christ told his disciples that he would send to them the Holy Breath, he may have been referring to initiation where the neophyte is touched by the descending spiritual fire. In the Mysteries the initiation process was often called 'sealing,' as it seals and makes permanent that which the initiate has attained. Paul, who both D.K. and Rudolf Steiner have said was an initiate, said: "And ye were sealed with the Holy Breath," and "He hath sealed us by giving of the Holy Breath." And in the Old Testament, 1Ephesians 1:13, "Having believed, you were sealed with the Holy Breath." And 1 Ephesians 4:30, it is said: "And grieve not for by the Holy Breath of God ye are sealed unto the day of redemption."[1] St. John in the *The Book of Revelation,* writes: "I heard the number of the sealed was a hundred and forty-four thousand." He goes on to say that the 144,000 sealed ones will be clothed in White Garments. And Ezra, the Old Testament prophet and probable author of the Tora, writes:

Rise and stand, and see at the feast of the Lord the number of those who have been sealed, those who have departed from the shadow of this age and have received glorious Garments from the Lord.[2]

---

[1] Ephesians 4:30
[2] 2 Esdra 2:38

The glorious white garments of the lord refer to the indestructible spiritual bodies of light. Origen (185 - 254 A.D.), the wisest of the early Christian Fathers, said:

> The material substance of the world, possessing the nature admitting all possible transformations, is, when manifesting to beings of a lower order, molded into the denser and more solid condition of the body; but when it becomes the servant of more perfect and more blessed beings, it shines in the splendor of celestial bodies, and adorns both the angels of God and the Sons of Resurrection with clothing of a spiritual body.[3]

In this very remarkable passage Origen is not only affirming his belief in the transmutation of material substance, but he is applying the transmutation process to one of its most exalted and useful conclusions, the transfiguration of the body into a spiritual body, not only after death but when "it becomes the servant of more perfect and blessed beings." Another important fact brought out in this passage is the existence of those 'blessed beings,' which he calls the 'Sons of Resurrection.' The Greeks have their Gods, the Mysteries have the Hierophants, the Buddhists have their Bodhisattvas, the Hindus have the Rishis, the Taoist have the Blessed Immortals, but except for the catholic 'Communion of Saints' very little had been given out in the West concerning the Divine Brotherhood, the Hierarchy of Beings who guide and protect the spiritual evolution of the world. Origen continues:

> But when this body which at some future period we shall possess in a more glorious state, shall have become a partaker of life, it will then, in addition to being immortal, become also incorruptible.

We must remember that Origen believed in reincarnation so that when he says that "this body at some future period we shall posses in a more glorious state," he is not necessarily limiting the period to this life.

---

[3] *First Principles,* Book 2, chapter 2.

In the Taoist alchemical classic, *The Secret of the Golden Flower*, it is stated that the new spiritual body, the Golden Flower, is externalized by a process called the 'circulation of the light' (light = energy). Master Djwhal Khul, in Rule 3 of his Rules of Magic, gives this hint: "The energy circulates, the point of light, the labor of the four, waxeth and groweth."[4] When applied to the human organism the 'point of light' here probably refers to the light in the head. The details of how the energy is to be circulated is one of the secrets of initiation, although the Chinese alchemists have much to say on the subject. On one level the energy circulates between the soul and its vehicles, which sets up a corresponding circulation in each of the bodies as well. From the *Emerald Tablet* of Hermes we read:

> *It ascends from the earth to heaven,*
> *And descends from heaven to the earth.*

Dr. Bacatrom, in his veiled commentary on this verse, says,

> *The Azoth ascends from the Earth, from the bottom of the Glass, and re-descends in Veins and drops into the Earth, and by this continual circulation the Azoth is more and more subtilized [spiritualized] (volatilized Sol) and carries the volatilized Solar atoms along with it and thereby becomes Solar Azoth, i.e. our third and genuine Sophic Mercury, and this circulation of the Solar Azoth must continue until it ceases of itself, and the Earth has sucked it all in, then it must become the black pitchy matter, the Toad which denotes complete putrefaction or death of the compound.[5]*

If we apply this activity to the human physical organism the 'Glass,' or crucible, represents the etheric body. The 'Azoth' is the vital psychic energy which is circulated through 'vines' or *nadhis* and refined through its contact with 'heaven,' at the crown. The 'third genuine Sophic Mercury,' the Philosopher's Stone, is the result of the third step in the condensation

---

[4] Bailey. *A Treatise on White Magic.*
[5] Quoted in Manly P. Hall's *The Secret Teachings of All Ages.* p. CLVIII.

process. 'The black pitchy matter,' the alchemical 'Toad,' is the old form, the earth, from which the volatile essence has been extracted.

The circulation and transmutation of the vital energy or chi within the etheric body is the subject of a very ancient (500 B.C.) Chinese alchemical inscription:

> *To transmute the chi it is (first) gathered and held. When full it is extended. When extended it descends. When it descends it ceases activity. When it ceases activity it crystalizes. When it crystallizes it germinates. When it germinates it grows. When it grows it is attracted upward. When it is attracted upward it reaches heaven. The secret fire of heaven attracts it upward. The subterranean fire pulls downward. He who acts against this will die. He who follows this will live forever.*

The rising of the flying serpent of the solar plexus is cryptically referred to in Taoist alchemical teachings as the 'Red Dragon rising from the watery abyss.' In the Tibetan Tantras she is called the Blazing Woman (gTu-mo). The Red Dragon, who is female, is also called the Thunder Dragon Mercury. The descending solar azoth is called the 'White Tiger descending from the court of fire.'

> *The Tiger leaps, the Dragon soars,*
> *The wind and waves are rough.*
> *In the correct position in the center is produced the mysterious Jewel.*
> *The Fruit grown on the branches ripe at the end of the season.*
> *How can the child in the belly be any different?[6]*

A similar idea is expressed in the *Golden Treatise* of Hermes:

> *The crowned king is married to our red daughter,*
> *And in the gentle harmless fire she doth conceive a son,*
> *Who is united most superiorly to this fire which gives him life.*

---

[6] Chang Po-tuan. *Understanding Reality*, Trans. by Thomas Cleary. Honolulu 1987, Part 1, verse 5.

The white seed of the sun enters the womb of subtle matter, thereby awakening the sleeping dragon. In the fire of their union is conceived the golden embryo of the child of the sun. An interesting analogy to the flying serpent or dragon can be found in Alice Bailey's book *Esoteric Astrology*.[1] She states that the constellation of the Dragon (Draco) is on a cosmic scale what the center at the base of the spine is in man. The Egyptians called this constellation *Hesmut*, the raging mother. In ancient China the dragon was used to represent primordial elemental forces. The dragon is not of itself a symbol of evil. The evil (the chaos) occurs when its forces are invoked without being able to master them in accordance with the evolutionary currents. To conquer the fiery dragon means to tame the raging elemental forces in one's self, in one's vehicles, in nature and the world. The raging mother must be mastered as it seeks 'its polar opposite,' at the crown.

The circulation of vital energy in the crucible is accomplished through the blending of the ascending forces with the descending forces, creating a radiant wheel of energy. This blending of these two forces (*prana* and *apana*) is spoken of in the *Bhagavad Gita*: "The yogi offers the *prana* into the apana, and the apana into the prana." The vital energy prana draws the energies inward and upward, toward the center. It operates under the Law of Attraction. The vital energy *apana* pushes outward and downward, toward the periphery. It operates under the Law of Repulsion. The merging of these two forces is called the 'chemical wedding.' The *Vimalaprabha*, known in Tibet as the Great Commentary from Shamballa, states that "the complete union of prana and apana in the navel is yoga, and he who practices this is a yogi."[7]

If we apply the science of analogy to the activity of the five vital energies of the etheric body, *prana* (intake), *samana* (assimilation), *vyana* (circulation), *udana* (transmutation), and *apana* (elimination), we see that the same laws and procedures apply to its dense counterpart, the respiratory-circulatory system of the physical body, though of course the details will differ. This basic circulatory process can be found in the

---

[1] Pages 45-46.

[7] 2: 108

physical-etheric organisms of all life forms, including, we are told, those of an atom of matter,[1] a human being, a planet or a solar system. Healers of the future will seek to gain practical knowledge of the etheric circulatory system, for it is upon this that the health of the body depends. In the future planetary ecologists will be seeking to heal the planet through an understanding of this same process as it applies to the vital energies of the earth. The key lies in refining the energies, balancing the pairs of opposites, and in eliminating obstructions.

The unification of polar opposites through cyclic interaction is a fundamental principle in nature. The serpent with his tail in his mouth is a symbol of this cyclic law in operation. In the rare book *Vadantic Raj Yoga*, we find a detailed description of the circulation of the vital energy within the etheric body (*linga sharira*). According to the accompanying brief biography the author, Swami Sabhapaty, was initiated into the mysteries by an immortal Himalayan Rishi. As the book was published in 1880 I have changed the spelling of some of the Sanskrit terms to conform with present day standards.

> *I now bring down the Universal Spirit in its fullness into the chamber of the brain, calling it the Spirit of Spirit or Paramatma. From the Brahamrandhara (center) it drops down or descends through the sushumna nadi (a hollow vessel through which the atma-prana akasha runs) down to the kundalini. This nadi touches on its way the eyes, nose, and joins the gullet with the alimentary canal, running along the latter it comes to the kundalini, where joining with the lingum and taking a bend upwards and ascending through the spinal cord or the backbone, it ends again in the Brahmarandhara…. Search after the Infinite spirit and its powers, which seem to descend and ascend in a circle.*

---

[1] See Babbitt's *Principles of Light and Color,* 1876. Not the inferior highly abridged University Books reprint.

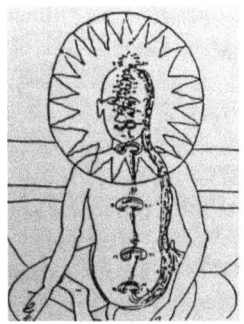

This sketch was drawn by Swama Sabhapty in 1880

The eightieth century Chinese alchemical classic, *Hui Ming Ching* by Liu Hua-yang, is introduced with the following verse:

If thou wouldst complete the diamond body without emanations,
Diligently heat the roots of the essence of life.
Kindle Light in the blessed country ever close at hand,
And there, hidden, let thy true self eternally dwell.

The diamond or vajra body is a term used in both Taoist and Buddhist literature to symbolize the indestructible diamond-like etheric body at any stage of its growth, including its glorious conclusion where it is said to be 'without emanations,' in other words no longer in the transmutation process. The 'blessed country ever close at hand' refers to the 'square inch space in the square foot place,' or the light in the head. To 'heat the roots' means to stimulate the organ that receives the incoming alchemical fire. The roots of the Tree of Life are above while the fruit of the tree are the manifestations of the vital essence as children of the sun.

The Fruit grown on the branches ripe at the end of the season.
How can the child in the belly be any different?[6]

---

[6] Chang Po-tuan. *Understanding Reality*, Trans. by Thomas Cleary. Honolulu 1987, Part 1, verse 5.

According to the *One Hundred Thousand Songs of Milarepa* many of his disciples, of both sexes, were able to manifest the rainbow body during their lifetime and therefore left behind at death no bodily remains. In the Isa Upanishad it is said:

> *May the vital energy (vayu) of the body,*
> *Now become the immortal vital body (amritanilam),*
> *Reducing this body to ashes.*

Shankara, in his commentary on this verse says that at this point of transformation process the vital energy of the body looses its physical limitations, attaining thereby its original nature, which is the all-pervading *amritanilam*, the immortal body of light. This amrita body he says is both the *sutratma*, or life thread, and the *Hiranyagarbha*, the luminous golden egg, the cosmic sheath of luminous fire mist from which a human being, planet or solar system is formed.[11] In the human kingdom it represents an oval monadic sheath of radiant Akasha, the Auric Egg that, according to Blavatsky encompasses all seven principles of a human being except for the dense physical body which is not considered a principle. On a planetary level it represents the *Hiranyapura*, the radiant 'Abode of the Resurrected Ones.' According to legend the Hirunyapura is symbolically represented by the Goddess Asteria, who due to the degenerate tendencies of humanity, withdrew herself from the world. She promised to return, when the time was right, to help humanity enter the Golden Age. The return of the Goddess, therefore, symbolizes the manifestation of the Hiranyagarbha or world Body of Light. The term Goddess is synonymous with the kingdom of the Devas, those subtle beings of nature who rule the third principle of psychic energy, the activity and power of mind. The pentagram, on one level, symbolizes the perfected Adept in manifestation as a body of light. H.P.B. gives a few hints as to the fivefold nature of the 'robe of resurrected Initiates.'

---

[11] Blavatsly. *Theosophical Glossary.*

The five words of Brahma, have become with the Gnostics the five words written upon the akashic (shining) Garment of Jesus at his glorification — the words 'Zama Zama Ozza Rachama Ozai' translated by the Orientalists, 'the Robe, the glorious Robe of my Strength.' These words were, in their turn, the anagrammatic blind of the five mystic powers represented on the robe of the resurrected Initiate.13

This may have been what Fulcanelli was referring to when he wrote of the 'matter of the Great Work *on* which the star appears.'

Alice Bailey writes:

Disciples are today witnessing the emergence of a solar characteristic, through the medium of their planetary Logos. . . . It is to this unknown and mysterious quality that the [five pointed] Star refers.14

Thomas Vaughn called the pentagram the 'soul-star' and the 'true Star of the Sun.'15 It is the light at the end of the tunnel guiding humanity, individually and collectively, out of the darkness and into light. St. Germain may have been speaking of this in his highly veiled alchemical classic, *La Tres Sainte Trinosophia*:

The hallowed bough which I had placed upon the triangular altar is suddenly ablaze. Its thick smoke envelops me so that I cannot to see. Wrapped in darkness, I seemed to descend into an abyss. . . . I was alone in a vast cavern, alone and far away from the whole world. . . . After walking for a long time I seemed to see a wandering light in the distance. I hid my own light and fixed my eye upon this object which I beheld... At last, after a long, long march I came to a square chamber. A door in the middle of each of its sides opened; they were of different colors, and each was placed at one of the cardinal points.

13 Blavatsky. *The Secret Doctrine.* Adyar edition, vol. 4, p. 152.

14 Alice Bailey. *Discipleship in the New Age.* Vol. 2, p. 326.

15 Vaughn. *Lumin De Lumine.*

I entered through the north door which was black; the opposite was red; the door to the east was blue and the one facing it was dazzling white. . . . I saw a star flicker and rise from its place, revolve, and then dart rapidly through the opening of the white door. I followed at once. . . . An invisible hand seized my lamp and placed it upon my head.

The bough represents the individualization of the Tree of Life. The 'triangular altar' represents the goal or focus, the spiritual Triad. The blindness is the so-called 'dark night,' the necessary and temporary withdrawal of the senses *(pratyahara)* from the physical world. The colored doors are the gates between planes. According to the Hindu Tantras the four lights—red, white, dark indigo (often translated as black), and blue—which one sees when one leaves behind the body and its senses, represent the four bodies: physical, etheric, emotional and mental, through which the pilgrim must pass (and leave behind for a time) to reach his Moksha (spiritual freedom). The red light is said to appear as the size of the body, the white light as thumb size; the indigo light, which is within the white light, is said to be the size of the fingertip; while the blue light, which is within the other three is sometimes described by seers as a 'blue pearl.' The concept of the Tree of Life, while appearing in the symbolism of many cultures, has similar characteristics in each. In the ancient Mystery tradition it was depicted with its root in heaven with its branches descending to the earth producing the gifts of spirit for the further evolution of consciousness. Through the Tree runs a mighty current called the Eternal Fountain, the Wellspring, and the River of Life. The water of this downward flowing river nourishes the holy seed and embryo, which after a time gives birth to the luminous body. In the *Book of Light* (*Sefer ha-Zohar*) we read:

It was in a manner the holy seed or germ that gave birth to the world, and is occultly referred to in the words, 'the holy seed shall be the substance thereof.' Its analogue in nature is the silkworm which, unseen and in secret, elaborates and prepares a product that ultimately constitutes the material of the monarch's purple robe of splendor.[17]

The 'holy seed' is the divine archetype of the perfected human being. It is the *augoeides chiton,* or auric egg, of Greek philosophy. The 'substance thereof' is that from which the 'monarch,' the initiate who has attained mastery of himself and the elements, creates (or better manifests) his 'purple robe of splendor' as a fully regenerated etheric body of light.

Fulcanelli said:

In the language of the Adepts, the term Golden Fleece [etheric substance] is applied to the matter prepared for the Work, as well as the final result [the luminous body]. This is very exact, since the substance differs only in purity, fixity and maturity.[1]

According to Mary Atwood,

The golden Fleece is the outward appearance presented by the light of Life diffused over the body of the seeker in the third life, it is of a purplish luster.[18]

Atwood gave this remarkable statement in answer to some questions raised by some of her students in her latter years. 'The third life' is undoubtedly a veiled reference to the third initiation, also called the doorway to the Greater Mysteries. Each initiation into the Mysteries opens the initiate to a new and greatly expanded experience of life and consciousness. At the third initiation, we are told, clairvoyant vision is awakened and the initiate sees into the higher worlds. The color of the etheric body is generally described as being golden probably due to the radiance of the golden prana that circulates through it, though from a higher perspective it seems to take on a more violet or 'purplish luster.' James Pryse, in his illuminating commentary on St. John's Apocalypse from

---

[17] *The Zohar.* de Manar translation, Wizard's Bookshelf 1978, p. 86

[1] Pages 152-153

[18] *A Suggestive Inquiry into the Hermetic Mystery.* Belfast 1918, p. 564

the point of view of the individual disciple, *The Apocalypse Unveiled*, gives the following description of the etheric body:

> In appearance it has a silvery luster, tinged with delicate violet; and its aura is of palest blue, with an interchanging play of all the prismatic colors, rendering it iridescent.

The violet color may have a connection with the fact that the etheric body is produced by the *Agnichaitans*, or Violet Devas, whose job, says Master D.K., is to weave from the ethereal substance of their own bodies the vital bodies of all living organisms. And in the Odyssey of Homer we read:

> On which the Nymphs amazing webs display,
> Of purple hue, and exquisite array.1

The following excerpt is from *The Dionysian Artificers*, an extraordinary document on the Greek Mysteries written by Hippolyto Joseph de Costa in 1820. Manly P. Hall rescued it from the obscurity of the Masonic Grand Lodge Library in Cedar Rapids, Iowa and published it through the Philosophical Research Society. De Costa is describing the ceremony of admission into the Eleusinian Mysteries, where the candidate, 'clothed in a sheep's skin or purple veil,' stands before three persons representing the sun, moon, and the revealer of the sacred secrets:

> *The Mysteries were not communicated all at once but in gradations in three different parts... These ceremonies, as I have described them thus far, appear to contain the lesser mysteries, or the first and second stages of the candidate's progress through the course of his initiations. There was however a third stage, when the candidate himself was made to symbolically approach death and return to life.*

---

1 *The Odyssey* of Homer.

The 'third initiation,' as numbered by Master D.K., marks the entrance to the Greater Mysteries. The title 'Initiate' is usually reserved for those who have entered the Greater Mysteries. Death and resurrection are central themes in the initiation process.

He who desires in pomp the sacred dress,
The Sun's resplendent body to express,
Should first a veil assume of purple bright.
Like fair white beams combined with fiery light.[1]

According to the *Secret of the Golden Flower:*

After a hundred days there develops by itself in the middle of the Light, a point of the true light-pole. Suddenly there develops the seed-pearl. It is as if a man and a woman embraced and conception took place. Then one must be quite still in order to await it. . . . When Life-Elixir-Pearl is finished, the holy embryo can be formed; then the work must be directed to the warming and nourishing the spiritual embryo.[2]

The 'point of tension,' the descending Light, the seed-pearl, the 'life-elixir-pearl, the holy embryo, and finally the Golden Flower itself all refer to steps of that alchemical process which culminates in the attainment of the immortal body of radiant Fire. Conception refers to the chemical wedding between the Crowned King and the Red Daughter, or as the Gnostics symbolized it:

While the blood flows from the blessed wounds of Christ and the holy Virgin presses Her virginal breast, the milk and blood spurt out and are mixed and become the Fountain of Life and the Spring of well-being. [3]

The mixing of the blood and milk, or the white seed with the red egg takes place in the crucible also called the Holy Grail. This blending, which results in the *soma heliakon,* is sometimes called the alchemical wedding.

---

1 Mairobius Saturnalia (Lib. 1. C 8):

2 Whilhelm translation, N.Y. 1935, pp. 34 & 33.

3 *Nag Hammadi Library.* N.Y. (1977) pp. 207-208.

"Without the marriage garment," writes Matthew, "no soul can enter heaven." In the *Book of Sophia* it is recorded that the Christ, after his transfiguration, appeared in secret to his disciples (7 women and 11 men) in his light body.

> *The Savior appeared not in his first form, but in the invisible spirit. And his form was like an angel of light. His likeness I must not describe. No mortal flesh can endure it, but only the pure and perfect flesh like that which he taught us about on the mountain of Olives in Galilee.*

Nargyal Rinpoche in his *Womb of Form,* a commentary of the *Six Yogas of Naropa,* informs us:

> *At the fourth and final stage of the path [the fourth initiation], the physical body is transformed into a Rainbow Body of Light. Through the eye of wisdom it appears as innumerable dancing colors like a crystal rainbow vase of light.*

The anonymous Master Mason and author of the *Ritual of the Degree of the Kabalistic and Hermetic Rose* says:

> *Be laborious like the Star and procure the Light of the Sages. . . . Matter will no longer have any power over you. You will, so to speak, be no longer a dweller on the earth, but after a certain time you will give back to it a body of its own, to take in its stead, one altogether spiritual. . . . Therefore, it must be revivified and made to be born again from the ashes, which you will effect by virtue of the vegetation of the Tree of Life, represented to us as the branch of Acacia.*

The 'branch of Acacia' is the microcosmic correspondence to the 'Tree of Life,' through which flows the 'Light of the Sages.' When this light, through labor, attains the degree of the Star, mastery of the elements and the birth of a 'revivified' spiritual body becomes possible. The 'branch of Acacia' is the human central axis, the *sushumna,* the electromagnetic pole uniting the neophyte with his inner spiritual nature. The resulting 'vegetation' or fruit of the Tree manifests through the nerve centers as the 'Light of the Sages.' From the *Book of Light* we read:

> *Within the Tree is a light, out of which radiates certain colors. These colors come and go, never being at rest save in the Tree. They are not at rest when they issue forth from it and show themselves in the light which does not shine of itself but only on the side of holiness.*[22]

The 'Tree' here refers to the etheric body the transfiguration of which produces the immortal body of Fire and Light. The fruit of the Tree is the manifestation of the light (*tigle*) of the etheric nerve centers, which first appears to the inner vision as the so-called light in the head (*murdha jyotishi*). 'The light which does not shine of itself' is the dense physical body, for its energy emanates not from itself but from the 'Tree.' It is illuminated through progressive states of consciousness. According to the *Book of Light*, "The fruit and sap of the Tree of Life bestow immortality." When ripe through a purification of the consciousness they become spinning vortices of highly intense energy of various colors depending upon the quality of the radiation..

Master D.K. gives a description of the Body of Light:

> *The centers, when functioning properly, form the 'body of fire' which eventually is all that is left, first to man in the three worlds and later to the Monad. This body of fire is the 'body incorruptible' or indestructible, spoken of by St. Paul, and is the product of evolution, of the perfect blending of the three fires, which ultimately destroy the form. When the form is destroyed there is left this tangible spiritual body of fire, one pure flame, distinguished by seven brilliant centres of intense burning.*[1]

This rare event seems to have been witnessed and recorded in *Pistis Sophia* by one of the disciples of Jesus during his illumination:

---

[22] *The Zohar* 2:2a

[1] *A Treatise on Cosmic Fire.* pages 166 & 167.

And as Jesus was seated apart from his disciples, the light-power descended upon him and surrounded him completely. And he shone most exceedingly, and there was no measure of the light which was about him. And the disciples could not see Jesus because of the great light that was about him. . . they saw only the light, which issued from him as many light-rays. The light-rays were of different kinds, some more excellent than the others. Basically there were three kinds of light rays. The second which was in the midst was more excellent than the first which was below. And the third which above them all was more excellent than the ones below.

The fully regenerated etheric body is a direct manifestation (externalization) of the fire of 'Auric Egg.' The immortal Augoeides,[1] or solar body[2] (*somo heliakon*) as it is sometimes called because of its visual likeness to the sun, is of an atomic, non molecular, substance. The etheric body (*sukshma sharira*) is of a molecular structure, though of a much finer grade or quality than its lower counterpart, the dense physical body.

The Tibetan Dzogchen teacher Namkhai Norbu, in his book *The Crystal and the Way of Light*, relates several stories of yogis in Tibet who have attained the Rainbow Body, or *Jalus* as the Tibetan's call it, and who thereby left behind no earthly remains.

To use the metaphor of the mirror, the realization of the Body of Light means that one is no longer in the condition of the reflection, but has entered the condition of the mirror itself, and moves into the nature and energy of the mirror. Knowing how one's energy manifests as Dan, Rolba and Zal [the three fires or internal energies] one is able to integrate one's energy completely, right through the level of actual material existence. . . then, when one dies, one's body slowly disappears into light. . . . All that remains of the physical body are the hair and fingernails, which are considered to be impurities. The rest of the body is dissolved into the essence of its elements. . . . The Body of Light, or Light Body of a being who has realized the Great Transfer, are both phenomena which can be actively maintained for the purpose of communication

1 Αυγοειδές literally means oval.
2 σώμα ηλιακων

with those who have sufficient visionary clarity to be able to perceive such a body.[24]

Master D.K. noted:

Eventually this body of light becomes externalized and of greater prominence than the dense, tangible physical body. This is the body in which the true son of God consciously dwells.[25]

In the Mystery schools information on the descent of the Light of the Paraklete, the Holy Breath, and its manifestation as an immortal Spiritual Body (σῶμα πνευματικόν) of radiant beauty and power was given only to those few who were preparing to enter the Greater Mysteries. The reason for the secrecy is that it is dangerous to attempt this activity artificially (through external methods) or prematurely. James Pryse states:

This work has to be preceded by the most rigid purificatory discipline, which includes strict celibacy and abstemiousness, and it is possible only for the man or woman who has attained a very high state of mental and physical purity. To the man who is gross and sensual, or whose mind is sullied by evil thoughts or constricted by bigotry, the Paraklete does not come. The unpurified person who rashly attempts to invade the Adytum of his inner God can arouse only the lower psychic forces of his animal nature, forces which are cruelly destructive and never regenerative. The neophyte who has acquired the 'purifying virtues' before entering upon the systematic course of introspective meditation by which the spiritual forces are awakened, must also as a necessary preliminary gain almost complete mastery of this thoughts, with the ability to focus his mind undeviatingly upon a single detached idea of abstract concept, excluding from the mental field all associated ideas and irrelevant notions.

Mabel Collins, a student of Master H., gives instructions to students preparing to enter the Greater Mysteries:

---

[24] Namkhai Norbu. *The Crystal and the Way of Light.* N.Y. 1986, pp. 128 & 129.

[25] A. Bailey. *A Treatise on the Seven Rays.* Vol 1. p. 137.

Man can rebuild his physical nature and manifest his divine nature out of it only when he knows that neither it, nor the animating power within it, are his own, or even himself. When he knows this, he is ready to build his body anew and from within it a spiritual shape worthy of immortality.[1]

In the esoteric teachings of India the threefold Spirit, Atma, Buddhi, Manas, find a reflection in the three vehicles of the personality—mental, emotional, and etheric/physical. After many lifetimes these three lower bodies are finally mastered, spiritualized, and transmuted into their original nature, thereby allowing the unobstrucing manifesting the spiritual Fire onto the etheric plane.

There exists many different means for the rarefaction [spiritualization] of the dense body... The Agni Yogi, who has passed through fiery baptism [the descent of the Holy Fire during initiation] and fiery transmutation, no longer dwells in a dense body, because when the body admits [radiates] the fiery currents, its whole substance is changed [transformed].[2]

What is left is the Monad and the [consciousness] thread, the antahkarana, which it has spun out of its own life and consciousness down the ages and which it can focus at will upon the physical plane, where it can create a body of pure substance and radiant light that the Master may require.[3]

---

1 *When the Sun Moves Northward.*
2 *Fiery World* III
3 Alice Bailey, *The Rays and the Initiations, page 101.*

The Great Work

The movement of life proceeds from the constant changing of one element into another.   Louis Kervran

Before alchemy existed as a science, its quintessence alone acted in nature's correlations (as it still does) and on all its planes.
                                                            H. P. Blavatsky

Before each great epoch, space is filled with fiery formulas. Thus is affirmed each great beginning.   The Teacher

The Great or One Work, advocated by the Hermetic Philosophers, pertains to the natural hastening of the spiritual evolution of Nature. To the Adept this involved cooperation with the Way, the Tao, the Divine Plane, God's Will; call it what you will. Each turn of the great evolutionary spiral is accompanied by the natural and spontaneous transmutation of the old, no longer needed forms, into those that correspond with the new evolutionary impulses. Adepts of the Art attempt to hasten this natural transmutation by stimulating its keynotes within themselves and the world. They understand that material evolution is but a reflection of the more inclusive evolution of consciousness, which in turn is a reflection of the spiritual evolution of the world and the cosmos. They realize that the Great Work of the great Brotherhood of Adepts is to further this cosmic evolution, to cooperate with the divine Plan to the level that they are able to perceive it.

Humanity, as a major player of world evolution, now stands at the crossroads, between the old world and the new. Nearly everyone can be classified as either of the old or new world. A few basic keynotes to the evolution of the consciousness in the new age might be noted:

1) Synthesis—the realization the oneness of all life. The dawning of this realization can be found in all fields of human activity. Einstein applied it to physics, demonstrating the oneness of matter and energy. The popularity of the Fritjof Capra's landmark book, *The Tao of Physics,* can be traced to the fact that it seeks to demonstrate the inherent unity of religion and science. Many great spiritual leaders of this age, including H. P. Blavatsky, Hazrat Inayat Khan, Yogananda, and Baha'u'llah, have been instrumental in bringing to the attention of the world the truth that all world-class religions are approaching the same spiritual truths, though from different perspectives. All cultural movements, including those in the fields of the science, economy, politics, religion, and social interaction, that work to establish greater unity in the world are responding this evolutionary impulse. The goal this divine impulse for humanity is world Brotherhood.

2) Beauty—the beauty of forms, the beauty of higher truth, and the beauty of the Way Itself. According to Master D.K., this evolutionary impulse will make its presence felt after the year 2025. It will be discovered that the truth of beauty is not something arbitrary or subjective (only 'in the eyes of the beholder.') It is a spiritual principle with its own laws and conditions. According to Rudolf Steiner, as related in his highly interesting *Story of My Life,* the reason that the esthetic movement of the nineteenth century was a failure was because it was divorced of the spirit, it did not recognize beauty as a spiritual principle.

3) All is energy—physical energy, psychic energy, and evolutionary energies. It is taught in the Mysteries that the universe is one all pervading Fire, from the dense slow moving energy of matter to the subtle, high vibrational activity of consciousness and spirit. The Hindu religion affirms this truth using terms such as Shakti and the divine Mother.

4) Group consciousness—a shift of emphasis from the individual to the group, group activity and group identity. This is a higher turn of the

spiral then merely the group life of the family. It can be seen in the small groups of kindred spirits working in the world for the common good, activists such as Red Cross and Doctors without Borders, and for good or ill the rise of corporations and businesses owned and run as a group. This evolutionary impulse directs us to world brotherhood and the realization of that great Hierarchy of Adepts that guide spiritual evolution of the world.

5. The creativeness of thought. The influence of his divine impulse can be seen in the many new books that say that the health, or ill health, of the body is a direct result of our thoughts and feelings or that we can manifest our desires through thought. The key to the creativeness of thought lies in realizing the power of psychic energy.

6. Direct knowledge. This divine impulse behind this idea involves the transmutation of blind belief into direct intuitive perception. Belief is unreliable in determining truth. "I hold it true," says Albert Einstein, "that pure thought can understand reality just as the ancients claimed." This idea lies and the heart of the religions of the East.

Part Two

An Alchemical Anthology

Tubula Smaragdine

The Emerald Tablet of Hermes Trismegistus

True and without error, certain and most true;
That which is above is like that which is below,
And that which is below is like that which is above.

This pertains to law of analogy and correspondence, which affirms that the macrocosm or cosmic universe is reflected in kind in the microcosm or human world, which in its turn is reflected in kind in the world of biology and physics. This great law is based upon two greater laws, (1) the Law of Synthesis, which affirms the essential unity of all things and beings, and (2) the Law of Periodicity, which affirms that cyclic evolution has the tendency to repeat itself in kind on every greater and lesser 'turn of the spiral.' Namgyal Rinpoche, in his excellent commentary on the *Six Yogas of Naropa, The Womb of Form* , says:

> Of all the themes to be examined, the most basic and profound lies in understanding the correspondence between the human body and the Universal Dharma.[1]

And the great Hindu yogi Gorakhnath notes that:

---

[1] Namgyal Rinpoche. *The Womb of Form*. Ottawa 1981, p. 4.

All worlds in the Cosmic System, all orders of existence, all planes of experience, are to be found in some mysterious way represented within the fully developed human body."[2]

The law of correspondence lies at the very heart of Hermetic Science and is the master key to unveiling its mysteries. In nearly all the esoteric literature of merit the veiled correspondences are primarily between an atom of matter, the human body, a human being as a whole, a planetary system, and a solar system. In working with the correspondences it is useful to consider the true form and not its dense counterpart.

> *For performing the miracle of the One Thing.*
> *And as all things were from the one,*
> *By meditation of one,*
> *So all things arose from the one thing by adaption.*

The fundamentals of esoteric science, whether of the east or west, include essential *unity,* one life, one thing, the universal synthesis. The miracle of the one thing is that it appears as many. In the same way that all things in the universe was produced from the one by meditation, so the alchemist can adapt this same practice to materialize a new form through the power of meditation.

> *The father of it is the sun,*
> *The mother of it is the moon,*
> *The wind carries it in its belly,*
> *And the earth is its nurse.*
> *This is the father of all perfection*
> *And the consummation of the whole world.*

The one thing, here, is the greater Life in which we live, move, and have our being. It is that Life spoken of in some esoteric systems as the Planetary Logos. Its father or originating central essence is the Sun, the

---

2 Banerjea. *The Philosophy of Gorakhnath*, p. 137.

Solar Logos. Its material source or mother is the moon evolution, its previous form before its reincarnation of the spirit of the planet to the earth, its second mother or nurse. The evolutionary current carries it forward. Its completed expression in form is the perfection and consummation of the world, including all the lives contained therein.

Its creative power comes alive when turned to earth.

This concerns all that is contained in the idea of 'fixing the volatile,' which is a concentration or densification of spiritual energies into etheric form. It is also the idea behind the manifestation of the Philosopher's Stone, the densification of the subtle (etheric) body, and the creation of the Body of Light.

> *Thou shalt separate the earth from the fire,*
> *The subtle from the dense,*
> *Gently and with much wisdom.*
> *It ascends from earth to heaven*
> *And again descends to the earth,*
> *Receiving, thereby, the virtues of that which is superior (heaven) and*
> *that which inferior (the earth),*

The 'earth' here represents the 'dense' form. The 'fire' and the 'subtle' represents the internal vital life, that which holds the form together, gives it life, and also mysteriously seeks liberation from its restrictive form. To gently separate these two means to release the inner vital spark, the volatile essence, from the form, to be captured and hermetically sealed in a specially prepared crucible. This, together with its descent again into a new form, indicates the whole art of alchemy.

> *And darkness will fly from thee,*
> *And thou will have the radiant light of the whole world.*
> *This is the strength and power of all strength and power,*
> *Overcoming all that is subtle*
> *And penetrating all that is dense.*

Thus, through these wonderful adaptions, was the world created.

When the second aspect of the tri-unity ⚛, whether of an atom, a human being, or a planetary system, expands to the point where it becomes free from the limitations and conditioning of its own form ⊖, the link which exists between its central spark ☿ and the evolving form, is greatly increased thereby allowing the universal energy or 'light' of ☿ to spiritualize the whole. For a human being this light illuminates the mind, so that 'darkness will fly from thee.' This Light when projected into form is the strength of all powers. Thus one can 'overcome' (condense) all that is subtle, and 'penetrate' (transmute) all that is dense.

> *I am therefore called the thrice-great Hermes,*
> *Having Three Parts of the philosophy of the whole world.*

He is called 'thrice great' because he has attained to the level of the spiritual Triad generally given in Hindu and Theosophical literature as spiritual will (*Atma*), love/wisdom (*bodhi*), and intelligence (*manas*).

> *Thus it is finished what I have to say concerning the Great*
> *Work of the Sun.*

La Tres Sainte Trinosophie

By Comte de St. Germain

T he following is taken from the last chapter of the highly veiled *La Tres Sainte Trinosophie* (The Divine Threefold Sophia) by St. Germain.[1] It is concerned with the completion of the Great Work and therefore with the manifestation of the Body of Light. As with all esoteric statements of principle this work may be applied on several levels. The following interpretation, therefore, does not contradict the able commentary given to it by Manly P. Hall. We are grateful to him for placing this important work before the English speaking public and for his assistance in decoding many of its hidden ciphers.

I crossed the palace, and mounting on the marble platform that was before me, I noticed with astonishment that I had re-entered the Hall of Thorns (the first in which I had found myself when entering the Palace of Wisdom). The triangular alter was still in the center of this hall but the bird, the alter, and the torch were now joined into a single body. Near them was a golden sun. The sword, which I had brought from the hall of fire,

---

1 *The Most Holy Trinosophia.* Commentary and Introduction by Manly P. Hall. The Philosophical Research Society, 1962. St. Germain here is not to be confused with the author of many so-called 'channeled' works.

laid a few paces distant on the cushion of one of the thrones; I took up the sword and struck the sun reducing it to dust. I then touched it and each molecule became a golden sun like the one I had broken. At that instant a loud and melodious voice exclaimed, "the work has been perfected!" Hearing this, the Children of Light hastened to join me, the doors of immortality were opened to me and the cloud which covers the eyes of mortals, was dissipated. I SAW and the spirits which preside over the elements knew me for their master.

What may at first seem like a children's fantasy is in reality a kind of spiritual autobiography depicting symbolically the steps to be taken to reach the high rank of Adept. His journey on the Path begins in earnest as he leaves behind and the physical world, represented by the Hall of Thorns, and by following the Flaming Star, the *murdhajoytish*, through the astral plane to the higher worlds. His goal, which he attains in the end, is to unite in full consciousness the three seemingly separate aspects of his being—the spirit (bird), the fiery heart/soul (torch) and the single threefold personality (triangular altar). Earlier in the work St. Germain states that these three aspects are in fact symbolic of all things, and that nothing can be done without them. Generally they represent the Three Principles— Life, Consciousness and essential Form. For a person they depict the three aspects of his being—Spirit, Soul, and Vital-Body (the dense physical body is not considered to be a principle).

The passage under consideration refers to entering the Greater Mysteries. It marks the end of the soul's continual cyclic incarnations through the subtle planes and back again to the Hall of Thorns. The Initiate has united the three fires of his being, spirit, soul, and vital body and as a reflex the three fires of the vital-body, and has attained thereby the fiery will of the spirit, symbolized by the sword. Because of his attainments he now clearly sees the inner Temple of the Sun, which until now has acted as a bridge, uniting the pilgrim in the body with his own inner essential nature. Because of this the Temple of Jerusalem, which the Theosophists miscall the Causal Body, is no longer needed and is therefore destroyed. According to Master D.K. this takes place at what he calls the 'fourth initiation,' the key words of which are crucifixion and renunciation. As a result of the destruction of the solar body the power and light of the Auric Egg now reaches the vital body direct so that every molecule is stimulated, regenerated, and illuminated as a brilliant new Body of the Light.

Jesus may have been referring to this process when he said that the Temple of Jerusalem would be destroyed, and that he would rebuild it in three days, which he did. Rudolf Steiner says that the initiation process takes three days (some say three and half days). The Tibetans called this transfiguration process, the Great Transfer. The Tibetans say that the time between the destruction of body, inner and outer, and the creation of the rainbow body usually takes about seven days.[2]

The Children of Light, who now hasten to join him, are the members of the spiritual Hierarchy, who Origen called the Sons of Resurrection.

---

[2] Namkhai Norbu. *The Crystqal and the Way of Light.* Routledge and Klgan Paul. 1986,

The Ritual of The Degree of the Kabalistic and Hermetic Rose

Masonry, as Albert Pike, one the greatest of all the writers on the subject, rightly states, is an imperfect reflection of the Ancient Mysteries, 'the ruins of its original grandeur.'[1] The following *Ritual* is nevertheless one of the best examples of the true esoteric doctrine to be still found within the Masonic Fraternity. It demonstrates without question the fact that Masonry, has a very significant esoteric side whose deeper aspects have remained hidden, even to the present day. Although the author and history of this work is unknown to me, it was undoubtedly written by a genuine initiate of the Mysteries. It was quoted by Albert Pike in his monumental Masonic classic *Morals and Dogma*, pages 785-789.

The true Philosophy known and practiced by Solomon, is the basis on which Masonry is founded. Our Ancient Masons have concealed from us the most important point of this Divine Art, under hieroglyphic charters, which are but enigmas and parables to the senseless, the wicked and the ambitious.

He will be supremely fortunate, who shall, by arduous labor, discover the sacred place of deposit, wherein all naked and sublime Truth is hidden; for he may be assured

---

[1] *Morals and Dogma*, page 23.

that he has found the True Light, the true Felicity, the true Heavenly Good. Then may it truly be said that he is one of the true Elect; for it is the only real and most sublime Science of all those to which a mortal can aspire: his days will be prolonged and his soul freed of all vices and corruption; into which the human race is often led by indigence.

If we interpret this work in terms of the neophyte approaching initiation into the Greater Mysteries then the 'sacred place of deposit' is the vital body. Specifically it pertains to the center of that body where the seed of the new life, the 'True Light' (spiritual energy), is deposited.

Be laborious, like the Star and produce the Light of the Sages and hide yourself from the stupid, profane and the ambitious. And be like the Owl, who sees by night and hides itself from treacherous curiosity.

The 'Light of the Sages' is first perceived by the candidate for initiation as the *murdhajoytish*, which we have discussed earlier. It is a reflection, a correspondence on the etheric plane, of the descending spiritual light/energy of the Soul. Its signature is a five pointed 'blazing star,' which at a certain stage of the alchemical process, blazes forth to the eye of an illuminated clairvoyant consciousness, 'who sees by night.'

The realization of the necessity to hide one's point of attainment from the world is a necessary prerequisite for this level of seership.

The Sun, on entering each of his houses, should be received there by the four elements, which you must be careful to invite to accompany you, that they may aid you in your understanding; for without them the House would be melancholy; therefore you will give him to feast upon the four elements.

The 'sun' here represents the soul (Sol) on its evolutionary journey, step by step, through each of the twelve chambers of the internal zodiac, a lower reflection (correspondence) to solar zodiac, also called the Temple of Sol-o-mon.

In the Hermetic Mysteries the 'four elements' esoterically represents the four elements of the *prima materia* or etheric matter.

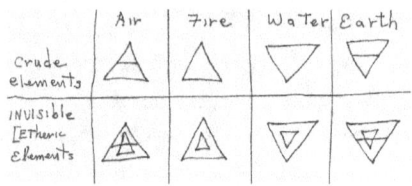

The four etheric elements, which make up the etheric body, will 'accompany you' on your journey providing the needed nourishment while out of the body.

When He shall have visited His twelve houses and seen you attentive there to receive him you will become one of His favorites, and He will allow you to share all his gifts. Matter will no longer have any power over you; you will, so to say, be no longer a dweller on the earth but after a certain period you will give back to it a body which is its own, to take in its stead one altogether spiritual. Matter is then deemed to be dead to the world.

Before the soul can begin to share with you its gifts you must be 'attentive to him.' This will take a high degree of inner sensitivity and self-mastery. Matter will then no longer be able to imprison you to the earth. Dense matter, and the forms it takes, will then be seen as a *maya*, an illusive reflection. It is 'dead to the world' as it has no life of its own.

Therefore it must be re-vivified, and made to be born again from its ashes, which you will effect by virtue of the vegetation of the Tree of Life, represented to us by the branch of acacia. Whoever shall learn to comprehend and execute this great work, will know great things, say the Sages of the Work. But when ever you depart from the center of the square and the compass you will no longer be able to work with success.

The branch of acacia is an individualization of the Tree of Life. The square and the compass are the tools of the master builder, which he uses to construct the foursquare *mayavirupa*, within the circle of the auric egg. At the center of the circle and the square is found the jewel. When one works from this point there is success.

To *re*-vivify, to be born again from the ashes of the old form, means first to return it to its essential nature and from there to manifest a new more perfected form.

Another Jewel is necessary for you, and in certain undertakings cannot be dispensed with. It is what is termed the Kabalistic pentacle . . . this carries with it the power of commanding the spirits of the elements. It is necessary for you to know how to use it and this you will learn by perseverance, if you are a lover of the science of our predecessors, the Sages.

This jewel is a condensation of the 'Light of the Sages,' which St. John says is given to those who overcome. It is by projecting of this light that one gains power over the elements. The secret of the pentacle is found in its geometry. Its five points can be viewed as five central points within five interlocking circles.

The great Black Eagle is the King of Birds. He alone is it that can fire the Sun material in its nature that has no form, and yet by its form develops color. The black is a complete harbinger of the work: it changes color and assumes a natural form, out whereof will emerge a brilliant Sun.

The eagle is the 'heavenly flyer' of Hermes, which when released from the confines of form opens a channel to the Light to the philosophical Sun. The black color represents its nature before transmutation through the spectrum of colors to its essential nature, the white light of the *prima materia*. The 'brilliant sun,' that is to emerge, is the Body of Light.

The birth of the Sun is always announced by its Star, represented by the Blazing Star, which you will know by its fiery color; and it is followed in its course by the silvery luster of the moon.

A rough Ashlar is the shapeless stone which is to be prepared in order to commence the philosophical work; and to be developed, in order to change its form from triangular to cubic, after the separation from it of its Salt, Sulphur and Mercury, by aid of the Square, Level, and balance and all the other Masonic implements which we use symbolically.

In esoteric Masonry the 'philosophical work' consists in the transmutation of the 'rough Ashlar' into the perfect Ashlar. The Ashlar is a human condensation of the element of the sun. Materialization is brought about by changing the vibrational rate along with its geometric pattern from triangular to cubic, from spiritual to physical, thereby stepping down very subtle energy into physical manifestation. This is a great mystery. Salt, Sulphur and Mercury are symbols representing the three subtle aspects or qualities of living matter.

Here we put them to philosophical use, to constitute a well-proportioned edifice, through which you are to make pass the crude material analogous to a candidate commencing his initiation into the Mysteries.

The 'philosophical use' of the three principles is accomplished through the agency of the 'Masonic implements' used to build 'a well proportioned edifice.' The process takes place as the 'candidate prepares for initiation into the Mysteries,' sometimes called the 'third initiation.' As we have stated above there is a direct correspondence between the transformation of the consciousness and its vehicles through the application of the Rod of Initiation and the transmutation of matter into a new higher form through the application of the Philosopher's Stone. The 'well-proportioned edifice' is the blueprints for the spiritual Temple, the geometrical prototype to which the *materia lucida* must conform and from which the temple is to be formed. It sounds the keynote or seed vibration for the manifestation of the new form. For an Adept the new form is the *mayavirupa*. For the master alchemist it is the Philosopher's Stone.

When we build we must observe all the rules and proportions; for other wise the Spirit of Life cannot lodge therein. So you will build the great tower, in which is to burn the fire of the Sages, or, in other words the fire of Heaven; as also the Sea of the Sages, in which the sun and moon are to be bathed. This is the basin of purification, in which will be the water of Celestial Grace, water that doth not soil the hands, but purifies all leprous bodies.

The 'spirit of life' is the volatile essence that has been abstracted from the old form in order that it may now be lodged in a greater form. This transfer of the central spark must take place without it being lost. It must therefore must be 'hermetically sealed' in its own 'ring pas not.' The 'great tower,' along which the light ascends and descends, is the *axis mundi*, which unites heaven and earth. When applied in the human arena it has been called the *sutratma, sushumna,* and *antahkarana,* the life thread, the creative thread, and consciousness thread. The Hermetic philosopher's symbolized this with the Staff of Hermes.

It is the fire of the sages that ascends the central axis and is purified of 'leprous bodies' through contact with the now intensified points of tension. It is nourishment by the 'water of celestial grace' (psychic energy) drawn from the 'sea of the sages,' also known as the 'lake of fire,' the mind of the alchemist.

Let us labor to instruct our Brother to the end that by his toils he may succeed in discovering the principle of life contained in the profundity of matter, known by the name of Alkahest.

The alkahest or universal solvent is the life giving principle found within the essence of matter. It dissolves and transmutes matter back into its original condition.

The most potent of the names of Deity is Adonai. Its power is to put the universe in movement; and the Knights who shall be fortunate enough to possess it, shall have at their disposition all the potencies that man is capable of knowing. By its power they would succeed in discovering the primary metal of the sun, which holds within itself the

127

principle of the germ, and where with we can put in alliance and six other metals, each of which contains the principles and primary seed of the grand philosophical Work.

The ancient sages tell us that Adonai is the spiritual Sun. The Knights of the Sun are the Initiates of the Greater Mysteries who have mastered the elements (elementals) both internal and external. The germ or seed of the sun, the philosophical gold, is the basis or foundation of the work of the Builders and is common to the other six metals. The 'seven metals of the sun' are symbols for the seven root substances from which all manifested forms are built and on a higher turn of the spiral, the seven primary energies of this world system.

The six other metals are Saturn, Jupiter, Mars, Venus, Mercury, and Luna; vulgarly known as Lead, Tin, Copper, Quicksilver and Silver. Gold is not included because it is not in its nature a metal. It is all spirit and incorruptible; wherefore it is the emblem of the Sun, which presides over the Light.

The seven metals of alchemical literature, which corresponds to the seven sacred planets and the seven basic evolutionary currents or rays, basically represent the seven primary qualities of etheric substance.

The vivifying spirit, called the Alkahest has in itself the generative virtue of producing the triangular cubic stone and contains in itself all the virtues to render men happy in this world and in that to come. To arrive at the composition of that Alkahest, we begin by laboring at the science of the union of the four elements, which are to be obtained from the three Kingdoms of nature, the mineral, vegetable and the animal. The rule, measure, weight and equipoise whereof have each their key. We then employ in one work the animals, vegetables and minerals, each in his season, which make the space of the House of the Sun, where they have all the virtues required.

The Alkahest, the universal solvent, is that elemental fire or energy that dissolves the elements into their essential nature, which is the common quintessence of the 'four elements.' This transmutation process, which can be applied to any of the kingdoms of nature, including the human, is symbolically called 'the union of the four elements.' Its 'generative virtue' lies in clothing the 'jewel,' the *prima materia* or first matter, once extracted, into a new form through the 'triangular cubic stone,' the blueprint of both extraction and materialization.

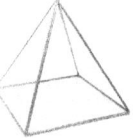

Our Stone, which has five points of tension, is a mathematical representation of the quintessence of etheric matter (*prima materia*) manifesting into form. This is symbolized in the forth and fifth hieroglyph of the Book of Hermes.[1] The dodecahedron crystal represents a further manifestation of the philosophical Stone produced through a condensation of the element of the sun.

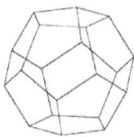

The 'House of the Sun,' here represents the Temple of Sol-o-mon, the Temple of Sol (the sun) in man. This internal zodiac, which is a microcosmic reflection of the celestial and planetary zodiac, has twelve houses or petals (whorls of spiral rotation).

Something from each of the three Kingdoms of Nature is assigned to each Celestial House, to the end that everything may be done in accordance with sound philosophical rules; and that everything may be presented at the wedding-table of the Spouse and the six virgins who hold the mystic shovel, without a common fire, but with an elemental fire, that comes primarily by attraction and by digestion in the philosophical bed lighted by the four elements.

---

[1] See my *The Book of Hermes*, Pentarba Publications, 2018

In the human kingdom the alchemical wedding is that unification of the consciousness, the higher with the lower, that takes place at initiation. 'The spouse and the six virgins' bring to the wedding table a unification of the seven principles or primary energies of Nature (*manas*). The 'mystic shovel' is given as a clue as to where these energies are to be united—the mystical earth—the place where the 'elementary fire' of the four elements are radiant with light. Transmutation occurs through the unification and stimulation (at the 'wedding-table) of the primary energies of any system, (7 to 3 and 3 to 1), plus the attraction and assimilation (digestion) of the elementary fire on one level and the so-called Fire of Space on another. The term wedding-table, is the place of initiation, which has a corresponding meaning in the cosmos, in biology and the atomic world of physics.

At the banquet of the Spouses, the viands, being thoroughly purified are served in Salt, Sulphur, Spirit, and Oil; a sufficient quantity thereof is taken every month and therewith is compounded, by means of the Balance of Solomon, the Alkahest, to serve the Spouses when they are laid on the nuptial bed, there to engender their embryo, producing for the human race immense treasures, that will last as long as the world endures

Few are capable of engaging in this Work. Only the true Free Masons may of right aspire to it; and even of them, very few are worthy to attain it, and of the pentacle of Solomon, which teaches how to labor at the Great Work.

The weight raised by Solomon with his balance is 1,2,3,4,5; which contains 25 times unity, 2 multiplied by 2; 3 multiplied by 3; 4 multiplied by 4; 5 multiplied by 5; and once 9; these numbers thus involving the square of 5 and 2, the cube of 2, the square of the square of 2, and the square of 3.

Stages in the Magical Work

Translated by Master Djwhal Khul

The following is taken from an unidentified ancient proclamation found in the archives of the Brotherhood. It deals with a stage in the Great Work where magical thought-forms are created in order to dispel illusion in the three worlds, through thought, light and sound. It is included in Alice Bailey's *A Treatise on White Magic,* page 618.

Let the magician stand upon the mountain top.

In the symbolic language of the Mysteries the mountain usually represents the mind. The mountain top is the essence of mind, the highest point upon the mental plane.

Beneath him in the valleys and the plains, water and streams and clouds are seen.

Below the plane of mind is the emotional and physical planes. Water here symbolizes emotion. The streams are the emotional currents and the clouds are emotions tinged with mind (*kama-manas*). The magician must have risen above both the pull of the emotions and the distractions of the physical senses, in order to obtain the clear vision necessary for true creative work.

Above him is the blue of heaven, the radiance of the rising sun, the pureness of the mountain air.

The blue of heaven is the intuitional plane, the purified and refined consciousness of love/wisdom, through which the rising sun, the incoming rays of the spiritual light of the Monad, the One, is seen.

Each sound is clear, The silence speaks with sound.

Not only does the magician hear of the Voice of Silence, the subtle vibration of the indwelling spirit, but he sounds it in unison.

Let the magician stand within the sun; looking from thence upon the ball of earth.

The magician here identifies with his true nature, the spiritual sun within, thus placing the earthly body, the 'not self,' in clear perspective. In this way the magician gains an objective perspective of the world, one not colored by false identification with it.

From that high point of peace serene let him sound forth the words that will create the forms, build worlds and universes and give life to that which he has made.

From this high point, the watery emotional element, has been stabilized and at peace, for it is said that 'truth disappears in water.' With clear vision and a mastery of the mind, he creates the necessary thought-forms, through image, sound, and rhythm, drawing the purpose and will from the hidden archetypes of the divine Plan.

According to one of the fundamental creative laws of Nature thoughts, if vital and clear, have a tendency to manifest in some way onto physical plain. The activity of the consciousness is reflected in the thought producing mind, which in turn is reflected in kind in events. This is the basis of karma. It is also one of the primary methods of service as a white magician. To keep alive the thought-forms, even after he has withdrawn the energy of his attention, the magician must give livingness as a spark from his own life flame.

Let him project the forms created on the mountain top in such a way that they cleave the clouds which circle round the ball of earth, and carry light and power. These dispel the veil of the forms which hide the true abode from the eye of the beholder.

The clouds are the veils of maya, of illusion. They must be dispelled from the mountain top, from the highest point of the mind, without any emotional attachment, so that the clear light of truth may be seen by all. The single eye of vision is creative as well as receptive.

Aula Lucis

The House of Light

By Thomas Vaughn

Thomas Vaughn (1621-1666), a student of the Rosicrucian Brotherhood, was careful not to disclose dangerous secrets to the general public. "For my own part," he tells us, "I shall observe a mean [middle] way, neither too obscure nor too open, but such as may serve posterity and add some splendor to the science itself." His *Aula Lucis*, from which the following extract is taken, pertains to a central Hermetic Mystery, the natural crystallization of the spiritual Light in the subtle body and its full expression as a radiant Body of Light. Vaughn symbolizes this immortal body as a 'House of Light.'

Light originally had no other birth than manifestation, for it was not made but discovered. It is properly the life of everything, and it is that which acts in all particulars; but the communion thereof with First Matter was celebrated by a general contract before any particulars were made.

Light, or radiant energy, is not created. It is manifested, materialized from a higher source. In this case it represents the livingness, the fiery spark, of material nature.

The matter, of itself, was a passive thin substance but apt to retain light, as smoke is to retain flame. After impregnation it is condensed to a crystalline moisture, unctuous and fiery, of nature hermaphroditical, and this in a double sense, in relation to a double center — celestial and terrestrial.

Matter itself is dead. It is the hidden light (energy) within it that gives it life. The alchemist works not with the form but with the subtle energy behind the form, either by extracting it from its dense counterpart or by increasing its inner activity to a point where transmutation occurs. To impregnate the matter with subtle energy (light) is to begin to crystalized it into that which is symbolically called by the philosophers, Stone. This involves the natural union of the masculine and feminine (positive or negative polarity) and can be considered in either the celestial or terrestrial arena.

From the terrestrial center proceeded the earthly Venus, which is fiery and masculine, and the earthly Mercury, which is watery and feminine; and these two are one against the other. From the celestial center proceeds two living images, namely, a white and a red light; and the white light settled in the water but the red went into the earth·

First matter, after it has been impregnated with the Light, is condensed or crystalized from the union of the red and white bindus, which is the earthly correspondence to the celestial spheres, Venus and Mercury.

Hence you may gather some infallible signs, whereby you may direct yourselves in the knowledge of the Matter and in the operation itself, when the matter is known. For if you have the true sperm and know withal how to prepare it — you shall find that the matter no sooner feels the philosophical heat but the white light will lift himself above the water, and there will he swim in his glorious blue vestment like the heavens.

The 'infallible signs' are direct though simplified reflections, in the form of geometric glyphs, which correspond to the natural patterns of some of the fundamental the activities and laws of Nature. 'Knowledge of the matter' is obtained through an understanding of these patterns. 'The Matter' here refers to the *prima materia,* which is the creative seed, the 'true sperm,' sometimes called 'Mercury.' To prepare the seed is in part to intensify it with the 'philosophical heat' of psychic energy so that it shines with a white light. When the white light rises from the fiery earthly Venus and the watery earthly Mercury, the manifestation of the goal of the operation itself — the glorious blue vestment, has begun.

But that I may speak something more concerning the chaos, I must tell you it is not rain-water nor due, but it is a subtle mineral moisture, a water so extremely thin and spiritual, with such a transcendent, incredible brightness, there is not in all Nature any liquor like it but itself. In plane terms, it is the middle substance of the wise men's Mercury, a water that is congealable and may be hardened by proper heat into stones and metals. Hence it was that the philosophers called it their Stone, to the end that no man might know what it was they called it so.

Thomas Vaughan here speaks of what he latter calls, 'the ground of all our secrets,' etheric matter, sometimes called the chaos. This subtle energy-substance is 'hardened' (condensed), into form, into the Philosopher's Stone, through the application of philosophical fire (psychic energy). We should remember that in all natural processes there is always a higher and lower correspondence.

For there is nothing in the world so remote from the complexion of a stone, for it is water and no stone. Now what water it is I have told you already, and for your better instruction I shall tell you more: it is water made by Nature, not extracted by the hands of man. Nor is it mere water but a spermatic, viscous composition of water, earth, air, and fire. All these four natures unite in one crystalline, congealable mass, in the form or appearance of water; and therefore I told you it was water made by Nature.

These are all hints concerning the fluid etheric energy-substance, the hidden water of life. There are four levels of this subtle biological prana that correspond to the elements, water, earth, air, and fire.

Earth and water are the only materials where open Nature works, for these two, being passive, are compassed about with the active superior bodies, namely, air, heaven, sun and stars.

Earth and water, here refer to the two lowest grades of etheric matter. They are receptive to the influence of higher energies and centers.

Thus do they stand in the very fire, at least under the beams and ejaculations thereof, so that the earth is subject to a continual torrefaction and the water to a continual coition. Hence it comes to pass that we are perpetually overcast with clouds, and this by a physical extraction or sublimation of water, which Nature herself distils and rains down upon the earth.

'Torrefaction' means to refine, purify, spiritualize. 'Coition' here means that the receptive feminine aspect of etheric matter has been impregnated with a beam or ray of the spiritual fire, the fiery seed. This intensifies, purifies and refines the etheric light-substance, which then Nature Herself distils, circulates, and returns, according to the natural evolutionary impulse..

Now this water, though of a different complexion from the philosopher's mineral water, yet hath in it many circumstances that well deserve our observation.

'Water' as used here is the stream of the descending etheric seed or sperm. Mineral water refers to a densification (manifestation) of the energy substance.

I shall not insist long upon any: I will only give you one or two instances and then return to my subject. First of all then, you are to consider that Nature distils not beyond the body, as the chemist doth in the recipient. She draws the water up from the earth, and to the same earth doth she return it; and hence it is that she generates by circular and reasonable imbibitions. Secondly, you must observe that she prepares her moisture before she imbibes the body therewith, and that by a most admirable preparation. Her method in this point is very obvious and open to all the world, so that if men were not blind I need not speak of it. Her water — we see — she rarefies into clouds, and by this means doth she rack and tenter-stretch the body, so that all the parts thereof are exposed to a searching, spiritual purgatory of wind and fire. For her wind passeth quite through the clouds and cleanseth them; and when they are well cleansed then comes Nature in with her fire and fixeth it in ente jure sapphirico.

To distil our 'water' is to extract its fiery essence. When that essence is given a new etheric sheath the cycle is complete and we have the complete alchemical process. The process being discussed here, namely the externalization of Stone and Light Body (one is a manifestation of the other) through the circulation of the vital fluid (referred to as water) in the etheric body, corresponds to, (1) the hydrologic cycle — evaporation, etherialization, precipitation and externalization, (2) the circulatory and respiratory system — wind- breath, water-blood, and fire-oxygenation of the blood. The distillation-abstraction process and the condensation-fixation cyclic process is accomplished by Nature by first uniting the body with that fire of Saturn. The condensation, or fixing the volatile, is accomplished through cooling effects of the Sapphire.

But this is not all. There are other circumstances, which Nature useth above ground, in order to her vegetables. And now I would speak of her subtler-raneous preparations, in order to her minerals: but that it is not lawful for me, as it was for the poet — "To discover things hidden in deep earth and fire." However, I shall not fail to tell thee a considerable truth, whosoever thou art that studiest this difficult science. The preparation of our animal and mineral sperm — I speak of the true preparation — is a secret upon which God hath laid His seal, and thou mayst not find it in books, for it was never entirely written.

'Deep earth and fire' pertains to the generative essence of nature. Its preparation is its condensed precipitation into form. 'The seal of God is laid' upon the candidate during initiation. This is often spoken of 'hermetically sealed,' and can be applied on several levels.

Thy best course is to consider the way of Nature, for there it may be found, but not without reiterated, deep and searching meditations. If this attempt fails thee, thou must pray for it, not that I hold it an easy or a common thing to attain to revelations, for we have none in England; but God may discover it to thee by some ordinary and mere natural means. In a word, if thou canst not attain it in this life, yet shalt thou know it in thy own body, when thou are past knowing of it in this subject. But because I will not deprive thee of those helps which I may lawfully communicate, I tell thee that our preparation is a purgation. Yet we do not purge by common, ridiculous sublimations or the more foolish filtrations, but by a secret, tangible, natural fire; and he that knows this fire, and how to wash with it, knows the key to our Art, even our hidden Saturn, and the stupendous, infernal lavatory of Nature. Much more could I say concerning this fire and the properties thereof, it being one of the highest mysteries of the creation, a subject questionless wherein I might be voluminous, and all the way mysterious for it relates to the greatest effects of magic, being the first male of Mercury and almost his mother.

The secret alchemical fire is psychic energy, which is the 'key of our Art,' on all levels—inorganic and organic physical, the human organism, and the consciousness principle, of which the purging, condensing, downward moving, fire of Saturn and the creative first male of Mercury (prana in the body) are aspects. As alchemy is a natural process, its methods and procedures will closely follow the 'way of Nature.'

Consider then the generation of our Mercury and how he is made, for here lies the ground of all our secrets. It is plain that outwardly we see nothing but what is gross — for example, earth, water, metals, stones and, amongst the better creatures, man himself. All these things have a lumpish, ineffectual outside, but inwardly they are full of a subtle, vital limosity [essence], impregnated with fire; and this Nature makes use of in generations, wherefore we call it the sperm. For instance sake, we know the body of man is not the sperm, but the sperm is a subtle extraction taken out of the body. Even so in the great world, the body or fabric itself in not the seed. It is not earth, air, fire or water; for these four — if they were put together — would be still four bodies of different forms and complexions. The seed then, or first matter, is a certain limosity extracted from these four, for every one of them contributes from its very centre a thin, slimy substance; and of their several slimes Nature makes the sperm by an ineffable union and mixture. This mixture and composition of slimy pronciples is that mass which we call the first matter. It is the minera of man, whereof God made him: in a double image did He make him in the day that he became a living soul. Hence a famous artist, speaking of the creation of Atom and alluding to the first matter, delivers himself in these terms: "From the essence of the elements did God create Adam, namely, from the essence of earth, water, air and fire. He gave him life from the sun of the Holy Spirit, which is the light of the world," Have a care that you mistake not any specified body for the sperm: beware of quicksilver, antimony and all the metals; and have nothing to do with aught that is extracted from metals. Beware of salts, vitriols and every minor mineral. Beware of animals and vegetables, and everything that is particular, or takes place in the classis of any known species. The first matter is a miraculous substance, one of which you may affirm contraries without inconvenience. It is vey weak and yet most strong; it is excessively soft and yet there is nothing go hard; it is one and all, spirit and body, fixed and volatile, male and female, visible and invisible. It is fire and burns not; it is water and wets not; it is earth that runs and air that stands still. In a word, it is Mercury, the laughter of fools and the wonder of the wise, nor hath God made anything that is like him.

The 'sun of the Holy Spirit, which is the Light of the World,' is primordial Energy at the highest level, the source and essence of all livingness. The 'ground of all our secrets' is the *prima materia* or 'first matter,' the 'minera,' or matrix in which the descending seed of spirit is planted, and from which metals or precious stones may be formed.

He is born in the world, but was existent before the world; and hence that excellent riddle which he hath somewhere proposed of himself: "I dwell" — saith he — "in the mountains and the planes, a father before I was a son. I generated my mother, and my mother, carrying me in her womb, generated me, having no use for a nurse." This is that substance which at present is the child of the sun and moon; but originally both his parents came out of his belly. He is placed between two fires, and therefore is ever restless. He grows out of the earth as all vegetables do, and in the night that is, receives a light from the stars, and retains it.

He is attractive at the first because of the horrible emptiness, and what he draws down is a prisoner for ever. He hath in him a thick fire, by which he captivates [attracts] the thin; and he is both artist and matter to himself.

The soul is 'born in the world' as the child of two fires, spiritual and physical. The 'horrible emptiness,' describes an intermediate stage in the transmutation/transformation of the consciousness. It pertains to the soul's exodus from the world of the senses, which temporally extracts the seed of spirit from the form. This invokes the Light of Heaven down to unite with the etheric body, to be absorbed and retained therein. The subterranean fire is 'thick,' while the thin subtle fire is the 'light of the stars,' the light of heaven.

In his first appearance he is neither earth nor water, neither solid nor fluid, but a substance without all form but what is universal. He is visible but of no certain color, for chameleon-like he puts on all colors, and there is nothing in the world from his accidents, he is water colored with fire, deep to the sight and — at it were — swollen; and he hath something in him that resembles a commotion. In a vaporous heat he opens his belly and discovers a azure heaven tinged with a milky light. Within this heaven he hides a little sun, a most powerful red fire, sparkling like a carbuncle, which is the red gold of the wise men.

The 'little sun,' the *murdhajoytish*, is produced through the alchemical marriage of the two fires, thick and thin, terrestrial and celestial.

These are the treasures of our sealed fountain, and though many are the treasures of our sealed fountain, and though many desire them yet none enters here but he that knows the key, and withal how to use. In the bottom of this well an old dragon, stretched along and fast asleep.

When the 'sleeping dragon at the bottom of the well,' is awakened she become the raging Mother (*Hesmut*). Her sealed fountain is unsealed.

Awake her if you can, and make her drink; for by this means she will recover her youth and be serviceable to you for ever. In a word, separate the eagle from the green lion; then clip his wings, and you have performed a miracle.

The eagle is the volatile essence, the heavenly flyer of Hermes, which during its exodus from the form must 'not be allowed to fly' on it own, i.e. escape from the confines of the Hermetically sealed crucible. The green lion is the body, the etheric form.

But these, you'll say, are blind terms, and no man knows what to make of them. True indeed, but they are such as are received from the philosophers. Howsoever, that I may deal plainly with you, the eagle is the water, for it is volatile and flies up in clouds, as an eagle doth; but I speak not of any common water whatsoever. The green lion is the body, or magical earth, with which you must clip the wings of the eagle; that is to say, you must fix her, so that she may fly no more.

To 'clip the wings of the eagle' is to seal it within an etheric 'ring pass not.'

By this we understand the opening and shutting of the chaos, and that cannot be done without our proper key — I mean our secret fire, wherein consists the whole mystery of the preparation.

Because of the obvious dangers, the key to the opening of the door to chaos, the primary energy source, has always been kept secret from the uninitiated.

Our fire is a natural fire; it is vaporous, subtle and piercing; it is that which works all in all, if we look on physical digestions, nor is there anything in the world that answers to the stomach and performs the effects thereof but this one thing. It is a substance of propriety solar and therefore sulphureous. It is prepared, as the philosophers tell us, from the old dragon, and in plain terms it is the fume of Mercury — not crude but cocted. This fume utterly destroys the first form of gold, introducing a second and more noble one.

In the revelations of the Mysteries fire and light are code words for subtle energy. Light is radiant energy. 'Our fire' is a subtle energy. The 'fume Mercury' is the radiance of the highest etheric energy on one level, and the highest psychic energy on another. The extraction of the eagle, from the old form will eventually destroy that form by removing its life essence that a new and nobler form may be manifested around that essence.

By Mercury I understand not quicksilver but Saturn philosophical, which devours the Moon and keeps her always in his belly. By gold I mean our spermatic, green gold — not the adored lump, which is dead and ineffectual.

The moon represents dense matter. Gold is a code word for *prima materia* (etheric matter) on one level and *prima lucida*, or radiant perfected matter on another.

It is well certainly for the students of this noble Art if they resolved on some general positions before they attempted the books on the philosophers. For example, let them take along with them these few truths, and they will serve them for so many rules whereby they may censure and examine their rules whereby they may censure and examine their authors.

First, that the first matter of the Stone is the very same with the first matter of all things.

Etheric energy/substance, a crystallization of psychic energy.

Secondly, that in this matter all the essential principles or ingredients of the Elixir are already shut up by Nature, and that we must not presume to add anything to this matter but what we have formerly drawn out of it; for the Stone excludes all extractions but what distil immediately from its own crystalline, universsla minera.

To distil is draw forth the essence. The essence of our Elixir and the Philosopher's Stone are two degrees of psychic energy that are crystallized into etheric matter.

Thirdly and lastly, that the philosophers have their peculiar secret metals, quite different from the metals of the vulgar, for where they name Mercury they mean not quicksilver, where Saturn not lead, where Venus and Mars not copper and iron, and where Sol or Luna not gold or silver. This Stone verily is not made of common gold and silver, but it is made, as one delivers it, 'of gold and silver that are reputed base, that stink and withal smell sweetly; green, living gold and silver to be found everywhere but known of very few'....

Each metal has a higher corresponding energy characteristic.

Matter — as I have formerly intimated — is the house of light. Here he dwells and builds for himself, and to speak truth, he takes up his lodging in sight of all the world. When he first enters it, it is a glorious, transparent room, a crystal castle, and he lives like a familiar in diamonds.

The transparent room, the crystal castle and the house of light all refer to the diamond (etheric) body at different degrees of transmutation.

He hath then liberty to look out at the windows; his love is all in his sight: I mean that liquid Venus, which lures him in; but this continues not very long. He is busy — as all lovers are — labors for a more close union, insinuates and conveys himself into the very substance of his love, so that his heat and action stir up her moist essences, by whose means he becomes an absolute prisoner. For at last the earth grows over him out of the water, so that he is quite shut up in darkness; and this the secret of the eternal God, which He hath been pleased to reveal to some of His servants, though mortal man was never worthy of it.

I wish it were lawful for me to enlarge myself in this point for religion's sake, but it is not safe or convenient that all ears should hear even the mysteries of religion. This leprous earth — for such it is, if it be not purged — is the toad that eats up the eagle, or spirit, of which there is frequent mention in the philosopher's books. In this earth also have many of the wise men stated that tincture which we commonly call darkness. Truly they may as well bestow it on the water or the air, for it appears not in any one element but either in all four or else in two and this last was that which deceived them. Now, the water hath no blackness at all but a majestic, large clarity. The earth likewise, in her own nature, is a glorious crystallized body, bright as the heavens. The air also excels both these in complexion, for he hath in him a most strange, inexpressible whiteness and serenity. As for a fire it is outwardly red and shining — like a jacinth — but inwardly in the spirit white as milk.

The earth in its own nature is the original or etheric earth, glorious and bright as heaven. the true four elements, the higher counterpart of the dense elements, are the four grades of etheric matter.

Now, if we put all these substances together, thouth purged and celified, yet when they stir and work for generation the black color overspreads them all — and such a black — so deep and horrid —that no common darkness can be compared unto it. I desire to know then whence this tincture ariseth, for the root of every other color is known. It is to be observed that in the separation of the elements this blackness appears not anywhere but in that element which is under fire; and this only whiles you are drawing out the fire — for the fire being separated the body is white. It is plain then that darkness belongs to the fire, for in truth fire is a manal of it; and this is one of the greatest mysteries, both in Divinity and philosophy. But those that would rightly understand it should first learn the difference between fire and light.

The higher counterpart of common fire (flame) is an intense electric energy or light. The flame, though producing an outer light, obscures the inner light, a light which reveals the true form and nature of things.

Trismegistus, in his vision of the creation, did first see a pleasing, gladsome light, but interminated. Afterwards appeared a horrible sad darkness, and this moved downwards, descending from the eye of light, as if a cloud should come from the sun. This darkness — saith he — was condensed into a certain water, but not without a mournful, inexpressible voice or sound, as the vapors of the elements are resolved by thunder. After this — saith that great philosopher — the Holy Word came out of the light and did get upon the water, and out of the water He made all things. Let it be your study then — who would know all things — to seek out this secret water, which hath in itself all things. This is the physical and famous Pythagorean cube, which surpriseth all forms, and retains them prisoners. "If anywise" — said my Companion — "a form implanted in this ground remain thereon; if it enters therein and doth abide in such solid receptacle, being laid up therein as in a material foundation; it is not received at random nor indifferently but permanently and specially, becoming inseparable and incommunicable, as something added to the soil, made subject to time and to place, and deprived — so to speak — of its liberty in the bondage of matter.

All physical forms exist only as extensions of their prototype, an invisible (to most of us) and subtle form made of the true water of the wise. The quote is by Reuchlin from his *De Arte Cabalistica*.

The consequences of this prison, which sometimes are sad, and the steps that lead unto it, are most elegantly expressed in the oracles. 'A steep descent extends beneath the earth, leading seven ways by stages, beneath which is the throne of a horrible necessity.'

As with many of the ancient philosophers who understood the true subject as well as the secret of correspondences, Thomas Vaughan easily switches back and forth between the mineral and the human kingdoms, giving minerals human attributes and human mineral characteristics. The form in the mineral kingdom is the prison house of its own volatile essence in the same way that the body is the prison house of the soul. The steep descent beneath the earth, refers to the penetration beneath the outer shell of matter, through the seven subplanes of the physical plane, to the throne of the first or original matter, the prima materia. For the human spirit the seven stages are the seven planes. The destiny of the human spirit as well as the volatile essence is fixed by horrible necessity.

The Philosopher's Stone

By Theophrastus Paracelsus

*F*or *sufficient reasons we call the Philosopher's Stone a perpetual or perfect balsam. Before it can be made through the agency of Vulcan it must first be known in what way the Stone may become visible and perceptible to the other senses, how its fire may be made manifest and recognized.*

The subject of this short manual is the manifestation of the fire [energy] of the Stone for the purpose of healing. The Philosopher's Stone is a radiant crystallization of the life-essence of the plant (perfected balsam) or mineral kingdom on one level, and the precipitation of the living-essence or psychic energy of a human being on another. The symbolic phrases, 'through the agency of Vulcan,' 'by the meditation of Vulcan,' and 'the art of Vulcan,' was a veiled expression used by Paracelsus throughout his writings to mean through an act of will. Paracelsus defines Vulcan as 'the living power of spirit.' Vulcan is the mythological blacksmith god who tempers, transmutes and perfects matter in the celestial fire. Esoterically Vulcan symbolizes the celestial impulse behind the Evolution. "Vulcan," says Paracelsus, "is the builder and architect of all things. His home is not only in the heavens but equally in all the elements as well." (*Lib. Meteorum.* e. 5) To be 'an agent of Vulcan' means that the alchemist initiates processes that are instep with the currents of evolution, the will of heaven.

To make this clear we will take the example of common fire. We will inquire how its force shows itself and becomes visible. First, by means of Vulcan, the fire is struck from the flint. The fire can effect nothing unless it meets with some substance that is congenial to it and on which it is capable of acting, such as wood, resins, oil, or some other like substance, which, by nature, readily burns. When the fire meets with such an object it comes actively forth, unless it be extinguished or hindered by something of a contrary nature to itself, or unless the material wherein it should multiply itself be deficient. For if wood or some similar substance be applied, its violence becomes stronger and operates in the same way until no more fuel is applied. Now, then, as the fire shows its effects in the wood, so the Philosopher's Stone or Perpetual Balsam acting on the human body. If that Stone be made out of the proper material and on the correct philosophical principle by a careful physician, and due consideration be given to all the surroundings of the man when he is exposed to it, then it restores the vital organs, just as logs on a fire. It revives the almost extinguishable heat, and is the cause of a brilliant and clear fire.

The term 'fire,' when used in conjunction with the human physical body, refers to etheric energy or prana. When expressed through the human constitution as a whole fire pertains to psychic energy.

Much depends, therefore, on the preparation of the Stone or balsam. But of more importance, before anything else, the true matter must be known and properly prepared and above all it should be soberly and prudently used. Such a medicine, then, should have the power to purge away all impurities of the blood and induce soundness in place of disease. . . .

The 'true matter' is etheric or dark matter. It is prepared for the work through refinement and purification. The manifestation of the Stone vitalizes the etheric body so that it may heal itself and eventually even bring about that condition called 'immortal.'

To do the subject justice I do not propose to romanticize or boast about the Philosopher's Stone. It is important, however, that it should be made of the proper material, and that is should be prepared and used with caution. You must know that many of the ancients in their allegorical writings have sufficiently indicated this material, and described the operation in symbolic language, so as not to disclose it to unqualified persons who would abuse it, and yet took care that it should not be concealed from their disciples. . . .

As we are to follow Nature and use only natural medicines, let us see what substance amongst those used in the medical art are most adapted to the human body for keeping it in soundness up to the limits of predestined death by means of their virtue and efficiency. If thought be given to the subject, I doubt whether any would disagree, that metallic substances are adaptable to the human body, and that the perfected metals, in proportion to their degree of perfection and especially the radical humor of those metals, can produce the greatest effects on the human body. For man partakes of that salt, sulphur, and mercury, which though hidden, enter for the most part into the composition of metals and metallic substances. Thus, like is applied to like.

The terms 'metals' and 'metallic substance,' refer to the essence of the metals, in fact all material substance. It is this subtle dark energy substance from which the stone is made. The perfection (spiritualization) of metals, we are told, in fact the whole physical plane, is one of the primary goals of the Great Work. It is accomplished through the transmutation of matter into its original essential nature plus the manifestation of that essence, the spiritual spark or Mercury of matter into form. This is brought about through the unity of the three principles, fires, or properties of matter, veiled under such terms as salt, sulphur, and mercury.

This process is useful to Nature but it must be applied in a practical manner. This is the great secret in medicine, worthy to be called its very arcanum. Is it any marvel then if great, unheard-of and unhoped-for cures follow, such as the ignorant believe impossible? I shall delay no longer, but shall set down here what I am determined to write in this treatise. I purpose to treat more clearly here than anywhere else the true medicine. First, however, it should be pointed out how much man obtains his origin from sulphur, mercury and salt, regarded as metals. But this I have sufficiently indicated in the Paramirum, and it is not necessary to repeat it here. I will, however, show how the Philosopher's Stone may be recognized, and by what method it is prepared.

Know, for a fact, that there is nothing so small but that from it anything can be made and can even exist without [a visible] form. Know that all things are formed, generated, multiplied and destroyed in their proper agreement with their original nature.

Once Mercury can be separated and isolated from its dense physical counterpart any new subtle form can be built up around it. But this primary form, thus created through the action of Vulcan, will be invisible or without any dense substance. The original nature, the etheric, is the prototype to which the dense physical more or less conforms and is materialized.

Thus it can be seen what each separate thing was in the beginning, and what it becomes in its ultima materia, its perfection. That which obstructs (this process) is a kind of imperfect condition, which Nature produces in the process of generation. The accidents can be separated out by the action of Vulcan so that they can be rendered inoperative and Nature can be corrected.

The discrepancy or distortion, which exists between the primary etheric form and its dense counterpart, must be corrected through the power of Vulcan before the perfection of matter can be accomplished.

This is what is done in making the Stone. Nature has made it imperfect, since she has formed, not the Stone, but its materials, which impede by accidents the effect, which the Stone, after due preparation, is able to produce. Such material, without preparation, is, as regards the Stone, a mere fragmentary and imperfect substance, which has in it no harmony. Alone it cannot be called perfect nor can it be used to heal the body. An illustration of this can be found in the microcosm. A person who, by mechanical power, is formed as a man only is not a complete and perfect work. He lacks harmony. He is fragmentary until the woman is created like him; then the work is complete. Each of these bodies is of the earth. The two together make the entire human being, capable of increasing and growing by the power of the indwelling harmony. So also with the Philosopher's Stone, which should regenerate man no less than metals. If it can be freed from superfluous accidents and be established in harmony with itself, it will perform wonders with all diseases. Unless this is done, all your attempts will be in vain.

That 'Nature has made it imperfect,' means that it is incomplete in the evolutionary sense. What is needed is to complete the process, to materialize and utilize that which is already a reality on subtler planes. To materialize the Stone correctly its vibrations must be in harmony with its surroundings. In a human being this harmony lies in the relationship of the centers. To find this harmony in a human being there must be a balance between the activity of the masculine and feminine (creative and receptive) energies as they are reflected in the centers.

If you wish to establish it in its harmony you must first reduce it to its first matter, so that the male may be in cooperation with the female, that the outer part may act on the inner and the inner be turned outwards, so that both seeds, the male and the female, may be enclosed together in complete concordance. By this and by the action of Vulcan they may be brought to perfection, and be exalted in degree, so that each, as a qualified, refined, and clarified essence may pour its virtue into the human body as well as into metals. Thus they will render them sound and will drive away any defilements by the process of expulsion. It [the Stone] will introduce, by the power of attraction that which is good into the blood, or any needed place, so that the microcosm, which is the outer world formed out of the [inner] world, may be led to health and kept therein. This it does by our medicine, not in the imagination, but rather by (attracting) that which is like itself.

The Stone, through the law of attraction, acts upon the subtle matter of the human body as well as upon the body of metals or plants. In the realm of dark (magnetic) matter, like attracts like and repels what does not correspond. Elsewhere Paracelsus states that the Stone attracts kindred, high vibrational matter to itself and to that which it seeks to influence, such as the blood.

This is the Mystery of Nature, and a secret that every physician should know. It can be understood by anyone who is well grounded in astral [etheric] medicine. I will now describe more clearly the nature and preparation of so excellent a medicine so that the Sons of Learning, who love truth, may be initiated. Know, then, that Nature has given a certain thing where, as in a chest, are enclosed 1, 2, 3, the virtues and power whereof suffice abundantly for preserving the health of the microcosm.

'Astral medicine' is an invisible etheric essence usually extracted from the plant kingdom.

The Most Sublime Gate

By Jacob Bohme

*L*ift up your thoughts and mind, and ride upon the Chariot of the Soul. Look upon yourself and all creatures and consider how the Birth of Life that is in you has its origin, and how the Light of Life that is in you, whereby you behold the shining of the sun, has its origin.

And look with your imagination, without the light of the sun, into the Vastness of Space, where the eyes of the body cannot reach.

Then consider what cause there might be, that you are more rational than other creatures,
seeing that you can search for that which is hidden in all things.

And consider further, from whence the elements fire and air have their origin, and how fire came to be in the water, and how the light in your body generates itself in the Water.

And then consider, that if you are born of God you will attain to what God is and to what the Eternal Birth is.

If you can see and feel truly you will find that all these must yet have a higher Root from which they proceed, a root which is invisible and hidden.

Look to the starry heavens which endures unchanging and consider from whence it proceeds and how it is sustained and is not corrupted, how it neither rises above nor falleth below, though indeed there is no above or below there.

Now if you consider what preserves all this and form whence it comes, you will find the eternal Birth that has no Beginning,
And you will find the Origin of the eternal Principle, the indissoluble Band.

And secondly you will understand the Separation of the material World, with its Stars and Elements, from the First Principle, which contains the outer world and the third Principle within it. You will find in the elementary Kingdom a Cause, which generates and moves all things. But you will not find the First Cause, from whence this is *so. There are, therefore, two Principles here [the first and third]. For you will find in all visible things a corruptibility, because if they have an end, they must also have a beginning.*

Thirdly, you will find in all things a glorious power and virtue which is life, growing and springing up of every thing, and you will find that therein lies it beauty and its joyful benevolence, form which is stirs. Now look at a plant or herb and consider, what is its life, which makes it grow? And you will find in the Origin, harshness, bitterness, fire and water, and if you should separate these four things and put them together again, still you would not find any growing. For if severed from its own Mother that generated it in the Beginning, then it remains dead, and you cannot bring back the pleasant smell or colors.

You will see, therefore, that there is an eternal Root that affords all this, for if you could bring the colors and the growing into it, yet you could not bring the smell and virtue into it. Thus you will find in the origin of the smell and taste that there must be another Principle, of which the stock itself is not a part. This Principle has it origin in the Light of Nature.

Now if you will look upon the human Life a little further, you will neither see, find, nor apprehend any more by your light than flesh and blood, wherein you are like other beasts. Secondly, you will find the elements of air and fire which are in you, and that it is but an animal or bestial life, for every beast has the same in it, from which proceeds the lust to fill themselves, and to propagate themselves, as do all the plants, herbs and grasses. And yet you will find no true understanding to be in these creatures, for although the stars and constellations operate in man, and afford him his senses, yet they are only such senses as belong to nourishment and propagation, like other beasts.

For the stars themselves are senseless, and have no knowledge or perception, yet by their operation on the Water creates a seething, boiling up one of another, and in the Tincture of the Blood, they cause a rising, seeing, feeling, hearing, and tasting. Therefore consider from whence the Tincture proceeds, wherein the noble Life springeth up, that the harshness, bitterness and fire become sweet. And you will certainly find no other Cause of it than the Light. But where comes the Light that it can shine in a dark body. If you say that it comes from the light of the sun, then what shines in the night and enlightens your understanding, so that though your eyes are shut, you perceive and know what you do. Here you will say that the noble mind leads you, and it is true. But whence has the mind its origin. You will say that under-standing makes the mind stir, and that is also true. But whence come them both? What is their Birth and why is it not so with the beasts?

My dear reader, if you are able, break open all and look into the pith. Yet still you will not find it, though you should seek in the Deep, in the stars, in the elements, in all living creatures, in the stones, plants, trees, or in the metals; also in heaven and earth, you will not find it. Now you will say, where then shall I find? Dear Reader, I cannot so much as lend you the Key that will lead you to it. But I will direct you to where you shall find it yourself. It lives in the third chapter of the evangelist St. John, in these words: "You must be born anew by Water, and by the Holy Spirit."

A True Concept of Alchemy

By Rudolf Steiner

We do not usually think of the works of Rudolf Steiner as being secret or veiled and yet there are some subjects upon which he either remained silent or what information he gave was in the form of hints. In the following lecture, given in Berlin in 1905,[1] he gave some hints on alchemy.

A true esoteric school is something very different from the usual schools. It does not start by cramming the pupils' mind with a great deal of educational matter. In a strict esoteric school the pupil receives no educational matter whatever, but is given a pregnant sentence filled with inner meaning and power. So it was in earlier times. The pupil had to meditate on the sentence in a state of complete inner calm, through which eventually he became inwardly filled with light, he became illuminated. When a person has advanced to the stage of perceiving his inner self, he can unite his consciousness with other beings. But for this he must have gained control of the point [of light] midway between the eyes and from there direct his consciousness downward into the heart. Then he can transfer his consciousness into other things; for example, he can then investigate what lives in an ant heap. Then he can also perceive the life in a beehive. Here however a phenomenon presents itself which is otherwise not to be experienced on earth. In the way a beehive functions one experiences something that is outside our earthly existence, something that is not found anywhere else on earth. What takes place on the other planets cannot be discovered merely by thinking. One cannot for example experience what is taking place on the Sun or Venus if one is unable to transfer one's consciousness into the life and functioning of a colony of bees. The bee has not gone through the whole course of evolution as we have. From the outset it has not been connected with the same evolutionary sequence as the other animals and man. The consciousness of the

---

[1] September 29th

beehive, not of the single bee, is extremely lofty. The wisdom of this lofty bee consciousness will only be attained by man in the Venus existence.[1] Then he will have the consciousness that is necessary in order to build with a substance that he creates out of his own being. The ants build the ant heap out of all sorts of things, but as yet build no cells. The building of cells is on higher planes something absolutely different. Through transferring one's consciousness into the beehive, through taking on the Venus consciousness, one learns something entirely different from anything else on earth, the complete recession of the element of sex. With the bees what is sexual is vested only in the one queen. The kama-sexuality[2] is almost entirely eliminated; the drones are killed. Here we have the prototype of something that will actually be accomplished in a future humanity, when work is the highest principle. It is only through the impulse of the spirit that one gains the faculty of transferring oneself into the community of the bees.

In order to progress further, let us now come to a true concept of alchemy. As late as the 18th century one could read in the German paper 'Reichsanzeiger' articles on alchemy. Kortum, the poet who wrote 'Jobsiade' was one of the most significant alchemists of the 18th century. At that time a number of articles dealt with the so-called 'Urmaterie' (primal matter), bringing this into connection with the Philosopher's Stone. Kortum, who was deeply immersed in these things, said at that time: To search for the Philosopher's stone is very difficult, but it is everywhere, you meet it every day, are well acquainted with it, you make use of it constantly, but do not know that it is the Philosopher's Stone. This is an apt description.

In Nature everything is ordered with infinite wisdom, with an infinitely wise economy. All living beings possessing Kama (astrality) — animals and men, and all etheric living beings — plants — are inter-related. We breathe in oxygen and breathe out carbonic acid. The animals do this also. Now if this were simply to continue, the air would soon be quite full of carbonic acid. But the plants assimilate carbonic acid and breathe out oxygen. Animals and men cannot live without plants. Now carbonic acid consists of carbon and oxygen. The plants retain the carbon and breathe out the oxygen. Man on the other hand takes in the oxygen and through his life processes transforms it into carbonic acid by uniting it with carbon. The plants build up their bodily form out of the carbon that they have retained.

---

[1] A stage of evolution to be attained in the far future.

[2] *Kama* is Sanskrit for desire.

In earlier times the appearance of the Earth was quite different from what it is now. Then, even in our districts there grew forests of gigantic ferns and horsetails, (equisetums). These disappeared. At first the Earth became covered with a layer of peat, the remains of the dead plants; then the former forests of fern and equisetums were transformed into the immense coal fields of the Earth. The rock formations developed gradually, either from the plant kingdom or the animal kingdom. When one looks at a lump of coal one can say to oneself: This was once plant. If one were to go still further back one would also be able to find the plants out of which rock-crystals, malachite and so on developed. The central zone of the Alps arose out of the primeval plants before coal. A diamond is exactly the same as a piece of coal. Nature has created the diamond from a coal still older than that which we have today. This rock crystal also has arisen out of plants.

Limestone is derived from animals. The Juras, for example, consist of such an accumulation of calcium. They were previously covered by the sea and are formed from the cast-off shells of sea-creatures. Thus the younger limestone mountains have arisen out of animals and the primeval rocks out of plants. The plant kingdom gradually passes over into the mineral kingdom. Everything solid on the earth has arisen out of a "plant-earth". This mineralising process can be studied through the development of coal out of plants.

The mineral kingdom in its present state of separation only came into existence during the Fourth Round. After this, the entire mineral kingdom will be spiritualised by man. He transforms it with the 'plough of his spirit'. Everything that man does today, the entire world of industry, is the transformation of the mineral kingdom. When someone quarries a rock in order to use the stones for the building of a house, when he builds a cathedral, all this changes the nature of the mineral kingdom by artificial means. In the Fourth Round man can work upon the mineral kingdom in this way. With the plant, on the contrary, he can as yet do nothing of this kind. The whole mineral kingdom will be transformed by man. To a great extent this will be brought about by oscillating electricity no longer requiring wires. Here man will be working right into the molecules and atoms. At the end of the Fourth Round he will have transformed the entire mineral kingdom.

From the Fifth Round onwards man will do the same with the plant kingdom. He will be able consciously to carry out the process that is now carried out by the plant. As the plant takes in carbonic acid and builds up its body from the carbon, so the human being of the Fifth Round will himself create his body out of the materials of his environment. Sex will cease to exist. Man will then himself have to work on his body, will have to produce it for himself. The same process of transforming carbon, which the plant now carries out unconsciously, will then be carried out consciously by man. (20) He will then transform matter just as today the plant transforms the air into carbon. That is the true alchemy. Carbon is the Philosopher's Stone. The man of the 18th century who pointed this out was indicating that transformation process, which is now carried out by the plants and which later will be carried out by man.

When from the higher planes one studies consciousness as it functions in the beehive, one learns how later on man will produce matter out of himself. In the future the human body will also be built up out of carbon; it will then be like a soft diamond. Then one will no longer inhabit the body from within, but will have it before one as an external body. Today the planets are built up in this way by the planetary spirits. From a being requiring a body produced by others, man will transform himself into a being who manifests himself through emanation. At that time he will consist of three members: 'Man in the evening who goes on three', as the Sphinx says. The original four organs have undergone metamorphosis. At first the hands were also organs of movement. Then they became organs for the spiritual. In the future only three organs will remain; the heart as Buddhi-organ, the two-petalled lotus-flower between the eyes, and the left hand as the organ of movement. This future state is also related to Blavatsky's indication (of a second spinal column). The pineal gland and the pituitary gland organize a second spinal column that later unites itself with the first. The second spinal column will descend in front from the head.

To arrive at such guiding threads as these, one must bring one's consciousness into a state of being that is at a higher level than we normally have at the present stage of earthly evolution.

All this was taught in the Mystery Schools and in a certain way, put to practical use. One must accustom oneself to developing one's way of thinking, and then one will develop in oneself a feeling that nothing is valueless, but that everything has its own inherent value. There is nothing in all Nature that we can obliterate through thinking without thereby disturbing Nature as a whole.

The ant heap also has a much higher consciousness than present-day man. The consciousness of the ant heap is to be found in the higher regions of the Mental Plane. On the other hand the consciousness of the bees is to be found in the higher regions of the Buddhi plane. How then did the ant-consciousness enter into our Earth? This took place through beings who stand higher than we do who had *already gone through the process of creating their body for themselves. Males, females and workers, the three members of the ant heap, comprise the body of a higher spiritual being. The human spirit also comes gradually to the point of dividing itself into three parts. Willing, feeling and thinking become separated in the case of the esoteric pupil. The molecules of the brain divide into three groups. The esoteric pupil must then out of himself connect a definite feeling with a mental picture. When he sees suffering, in order to experience pity, he must consciously add this feeling to it. To the front of the head lies the thinking part, above, the part of feeling, to the back of the head that of willing. The esoteric pupil learns to bring these consciously into connection with one another. Later these three parts become completely separated. He must then control the three parts in the same way as an ant heap controls the males, females and workers.*

Now we can ask why higher beings manifest themselves in an ant heap. But if formic acid had not been introduced, the whole earth would have been different. The foreseeing wisdom of Higher Intelligences was aware of the moment when formic acid had to be brought into the earth.

Thus we can gain a comprehensive understanding of the whole earth, so that we know and recognize what lives and has its being within it. This was the case with Paracelsus, who built up his concepts in such a way that he perceived how things could be used as remedies because he knew in what relationship they stood to man and his organs. For instance, Digitalis purpurea (foxglove) is connected with the heart and can therefore still be rightly used as a heart remedy. Nowadays new remedies are sought by means of experiment, in which one tests their effects on a number of people. In those days remedies were sought through intuition, because their inner connections were observed. Remedies discovered in this way always retain their effect, whereas with the others, in the course of time after-effects usually show themselves, which eluded observation when the experiments were first carried out.

From Infinity

Vol. 1 # 42

The assimilation of higher energies, upon the evidence of tension, can give from to new energies. Matter and spirit grow through mutual help.

The assimilation of the higher energies is dependent upon the creation of tension (intensity of energy) through one-pointed attention, such as in fiery striving.

The evolution of spirit, consciousness, and nature work through their mutual cooperation and interaction.

When the tensed current of will flows with accelerated speed, matter is absorbed by the spirit and the functions of the spiritual creator are preformed. Then the refining of form takes place.

The current of will is a directed stream of the energy of will, which stimulates the matter extracting thereby its essential nature, which 'is absorbed by the spirit,' and from which the 'spiritual creator' can manifest a new form in line with evolution.

The power of the fire of spirit is like the power of the fire that melts metals. Only through the process of melting may one form new combinations.

Subtle energy transmutes (melts) metals (matter) to be used to form new combinations.

That spirit who yearns to bring his energy in incandescence becomes the melter of matter. What forms and dimensions of spirit can melt, from all the spatial matter of our lives! From times immemorial the Lords have assumed the tasks of melting the consciousness.

For the term 'melt' substitute transmute. The transmutation of matter follows the same general steps as the transformation of the consciousness, not in details but in corresponding sequence. Here the consciousness become illuminated (incandescent), and thus the psychic energy as well. This takes place through the descent and assimilation of the fire of spirit. The forms and dimensions of the human spirit that can be transmuted are numerous. To melt the consciousness means to reduce (raise) it to its primary condition.

The Transmutative Process[1]

Master Djwhal Khul

The secret of the transmutation of the baser metals into gold will be revealed when world conditions are such that gold is no longer the standard and hence the free manufacture of gold will not lead to disaster and when scientists work with the life aspect or with positive electrical life and not with the substance or form aspect.

D.K.

Transmutation is a subject that from the earliest ages has occupied the attention of students, scientists and alchemists. The power to change, through the application of heat, is of course universally recognized, but the key to the mystery, or the secret of the systemic formula is advisedly guarded from all searchers, and is only gradually revealed after the second Initiation. The subject is so tremendous that it is only possible to indicate in broad general outlines how it may be approached. The mind of the public turns naturally to the transmutation of metals into gold with the aim in view of the alleviation of poverty. The mind of the scientist seeks the universal solvent which will reduce matter to its primordial substance, release energy, and thus reveal the processes of evolution, and enable the seeker to build for himself (from the primordial base) the desired forms. The mind of the alchemist searches for the Philosopher's Stone, that effective transmuting agent which will bring about revelation, and the power to impose the will of the chemist upon the elemental forces, which work in, by, and through matter. The religious man, especially the Christian, recognizes the psychic quality of this transmutative power, and frequently speaks in the sacred books, of the soul being tried or tested seven times in the fire. All these students and investigators are recognizing one great truth from their own constricted angle, and the whole lies not with one or another, but in the aggregate.

---

1 From *A Treatise on Cosmic Fire* by Alice Bailey, pages 475-484.

In defining transmutation, as it is occultly understood, we might express it thus: *Transmutation is the passage across from one state of being to another through the agency of fire.* The due comprehension of this is based on certain postulates, mainly four in number. These postulates must be expressed in terms of the Old Commentary, which is so worded that it reveals to those who have eyes to see, but remains enigmatic to those who are not ready, or who would misuse the knowledge gained for selfish ends. The phrases are as follows:

I. He who transfers the Father's life to the lower three seeketh the agency of fire, hid in the heart of Mother. He worketh with the Agnichaitans, that hide, that burn, and thus produce the needed moisture.[1]

II. He who transfers the life from out the lower three into the ready fourth seeketh the agency of fire hid in the heart of Brahma. He worketh with the forces of the Agnishvattas, that emanate, that blend, and thus produce the needed warmth.[2]

III. He who transfers the life into the gathering fifth seeketh the agency of fire hid in the heart of Vishnu. He worketh with the forces of the Agnisuryans, that blaze, that liberate the essence, and thus produce the needed radiance.[3]

IV. First moisture, slow and all enveloping; then heat with ever-growing warmth and fierce intensity; then force that presses, drives and concentrates. Thus is radiance produced; thus the exudation; thus mutation; thus change of form. Finally liberation, escape of the volatile essence, and the gathering of the residue back to primordial stuff.[4]

---

[1] The first postulate invokes the highest spiritual energy from above (the plane of Atma for a human being, the first (highest) ether when working from the seven fold physical plane) down into the three worlds of humanity (physical, emotional, mental) or the lower three subplanes of the physical plane (earth, liquid, gas) when working with the material. The Father represents the first aspect of the Trinity. 'The Father's life' represents the energy of the first aspect. The Agnichaitans work with the process of involution.

[2] Stage two raises the volatile essence of the lower three planes or subplanes to the fourth subplane (the 4th ether) or the fourth plane, the Buddhic. Brahma represents the third or mother aspect of the Trinity. Agnishvattats work with the process of evolution.

[3] Stage three raises the volatile essence up one more plane or subplane. Vishnu represents the second or heart aspect of the Trinity. Radiance means radioactive, to use a chemical term to represent a higher corresponding process.

[4] Stage four raises, through an act of will, the volatile essence, whether physical-etheric or the consciousness principle back to its primordial source.

He who ponders these formulas and who meditates upon the method and suggested process will receive a general idea of the evolutionary process of transmutation which will be of more value to him than the formulas whereby the devas transmute the various minerals.

Transmutation concerns the life of the atom, and is hidden in knowledge of the laws governing radioactivity. It is interesting to note how in the scientific expression 'radioactivity,' we have the eastern conception of Vishnu-Brahma,[1] or the Rays of Light vibrating through matter. Hence the usually accepted interpretation of the term 'atom' must be extended from that of the atom of chemistry to include:

a. All atoms or spheres upon the physical plane.
b. All atoms or spheres upon the astral and mental planes.
c. The human being in physical incarnation.
d. The causal body of man on its own plane.
e. All planes as entified spheres.
f. All planets, chains and globes within the solar system.
g. All monads on their own plane, whether human monads or Heavenly Men.[2]
h. The solar Ring-Pass-Not, the aggregate of all lesser atoms.[3]

In all these atoms, stupendous or minute, microcosmic or macrocosmic, the central life corresponds to the positive charge of electrical force predicated by science, whether it is the life of a cosmic Entity such as a solar Logos, or the tiny elemental life within a physical atom. The lesser atoms which revolve round their positive center, and which are at present termed electrons by science, are the negative aspect, and this is true not only of the atom on the physical plane, but of the human atoms, held to their central attractive point, a Heavenly Man, or the atomic forms which in their aggregate form the recognized solar system. All forms are built up in an analogous manner and the only difference consists—as the textbooks teach—in the arrangement and the number of

---

[1] Sound currents come under the influence of the second or Vishnu aspect of Divinity. Activity is the primary quality of the 3rd or Brahma aspect of the trinity.

[2] The Heavenly Men, as the term used in Mysteries, means those living entities or Gods Whose outer forms are perceived as planets.

[3] The goal of alchemy is to liberate the central life of the atom from its imprisonment in form so that it can latter be clothed in a new form more instep with evolution. This process can be applied to all atoms material, human, or celestial.

the electrons. The electron itself will eventually be found to be an elemental, tiny life.

The second point I seek to make now is: *Radiation is transmutation in process of accomplishment.* Transmutation being the liberation of the essence in order that it may seek a new center, the process may be recognized as radioactivity technically understood and applied to all atomic bodies without exception.

That science has but recently become aware of radium (an example of the process of transmutation) is but the fault of science. As this is more comprehended it will be found that all radiations, such as magnetism or psychic exhalation, are but the transmuting process proceeding on a large scale. The point to be grasped here is that the transmuting process, when effective, is superficially [only seems to be] the result of outside factors. Basically it is the result of the inner positive nucleus of force or life reaching such a terrific rate of vibration, that it eventually scatters the electrons or negative points which compose its sphere of influence, and scatters them to such a distance that the Law of Repulsion dominates. They are then no more attracted to their original center but seek another. The atomic sphere, if I might so express it, dissipates, the electrons come under the Law of Repulsion, and the central essence escapes and seeks a new sphere, occultly understood.

We must remember always that all within the solar system is dual, and is in itself both negative and positive: positive as regards its own form, but negative as regards its greater sphere.[1] Every atom therefore is both positive and negative——it is an electron as well as an atom.

Therefore, the process of transmutation is dual and necessitates a preliminary stage of application of external factors, a fanning and care and development of the inner positive nucleus, a period of incubation or of the systematic feeding of the inner flame, and an increase of voltage. There is next a secondary stage wherein the external factors do not count so much, and wherein the inner centre of energy in the atom may be left to do its own work. These factors may be applied equally to all atoms; to the mineral atoms, which have occupied the attention of alchemists so much, to the atom, called man who pursues the same general procedure being governed

---

[1] The greater sphere is the greater life of which it is a part.

165

by the same laws; and to all greater atoms, such as a Heavenly Man or a solar Logos.

The process might be tabulated as follows:

1. The life takes primitive form.
2. The form is subjected to outer heat.
3. Heat, playing on the form, produces exudation and the factor of moisture supervenes.
4. Moisture and heat perform their function in unison.
5. Elemental lives tend all lesser lives.
6. The devas co-operate under rule, order and sound.
7. The internal heat of the atom increases.
8. The heat of the atom mounts rapidly and surpasses the external heat of its environing.
9. The atom radiates.
10. The spheroidal wall of the atom is eventually broken down.
11. The electrons or negative units seek a new centre.
12. The central life escapes to merge with its polar opposite becoming itself negative and seeking the positive.
13. This is occultly obscuration, the going-out of the light temporarily, until it again emerges and blazes forth.

More detailed elucidation will not be possible here nor advisable:

It will be apparent, therefore, that it should be possible, from the standpoint of each kingdom of nature, to aid the transmuting process of all lesser atoms. This is so, even though it is not recognized; it is only when the human kingdom is reached that it is possible for an entity consciously and intelligently to do two things:

First: aid in the transmutation of his own positive atomic centre from the human into the spiritual.

Second: assist at the transmutation
a. From the lower mineral forms into the higher forms.
b. From the mineral forms into the vegetable.
c. From vegetable forms into the animal forms.
d. From animal forms into the human or consciously and definitely to bring about individualization.

That it is not done as yet is due to the danger of imparting the necessary knowledge. The adepts understand the transmuting process in the three worlds, and in the four kingdoms of nature, which make them a temporary esoteric three and exoteric four.

Man will eventually work with the three kingdoms but, only when brotherhood is a practice and not a concept.

Three points must now be considered in this connection:

Conscious manipulation of the fires.
Devas and transmutation.
Sound and colour in transmutation.

It is necessary here to point out, as I have done in other matters under consideration, that only certain facts can be imparted, whilst the detailed work concerning *process* may not be dealt with owing to the inability of the race as yet to act altruistically. Much misapprehension crept in, owing to this very thing, in the early days of hierarchical effort to give out some of the Wisdom fundamentals in book form and this is bravely dealt with by H. P. B. The danger still persists, and greatly handicaps the efforts of Those, Who—working on the inner side—feel that the thoughts of men should be lifted from the study of the ways of physical existence to broader concepts, wider vision and synthetic comprehension. Indication only is possible; it is not permissible here to give out the transmutative formulas, or the mantrams that manipulate the matter of space. Only the way can be pointed to those who are ready, or who are recovering old knowledge (gained through approach to the Path, or latent through experience undergone in Atlantean days) and the landmarks indicated hold sufficient guidance to enable them to penetrate deeper into the arcana of knowledge. The danger consists in the very fact that the whole matter of transmutation concerns the material form, and deva substance. Man, being not yet master even of the substance of his own body, nor in vibratory control of his third aspect, incurs risk when he concentrates his attention on the Not-Self. It can only be safely done when the magician knows five things.

1. The nature of the atom.
2. The keynote of the planes.
3. The method of working from the egoic level through conscious control, knowledge of the protective sounds and formulas, and pure altruistic endeavor.

4.   The interaction of the three fires, the lunar words, the solar words, and later a cosmic word.
5.   The secret of electrical vibration, which is only realized in an elementary way when a man knows the keynote of his own planetary Logos.

All this knowledge as it concerns the three worlds is in the hands of the Masters of the Wisdom, and enables them to work along the lines of energy or force, and not with what is usually understood when the word 'substance' is used. They work with electrical energy, concerning themselves with positive electricity, or with the energy of the positive nucleus of force within the atom, whether it is the atom of chemistry, for instance, or the human atom. They *deal with the soul of things.* The black magician works with the negative aspect, with the electrons, if I might so term it, with the sheath, and not with the soul. This distinction must be clearly borne in mind. It holds the clue to the non-interference of the whole Brotherhood in material matters and affairs, and Their concentration upon the *force aspect, upon the centres of energy.*

It will now be apparent that the whole process of transmutation, as we can deal with it at present, concerns itself with the two fires, which reached a high stage of perfection in a past solar system:

a. The fire of an atom in its twofold aspect—internal and radiatory.
b. The fires of mind.

It is with these that transmutation concerns itself from the human standpoint, and the third fire of Spirit is not at this stage to be considered.

This *conscious* manipulation of the fires is the prerogative of man when he has reached a certain point in his evolution; the unconscious realization of this has led naturally to the attempts of the alchemist to transmute in the mineral kingdom. A few of the older students right through the ages have comprehended the vastness of the endeavor of which the transmutation of the baser metals into gold was but preliminary and a symbol, a pictorial, allegorical, concrete step. The whole subject of transmutation is covered by the work of the Hierarchy in all its three departments on this planet, and we might get some idea of the matters involved if we studied this vast hierarchical standpoint, getting thereby a concept of the work done in aiding the evolutionary process. It is the work of transferring the life from one stage of atomic existence to another, and it involves three distinct steps, which can be seen and traced by means of the higher clairvoyance, and from the higher planes. These steps or stages are:

The fiery stage—the blending, fusing, burning period, through which all atoms pass during the disintegration of form.
The solvent stage, in which the form is dissipated and substance is held in solution, the atom being resolved into its essential duality.
The volatile stage, which concerns primarily the essential quality of the atom, and the escape of this essence, later to take a new form.

Radioactivity, pralayic solution, and essential volatility might express the thought. In every transmuting process without exception these three steps are followed. Occultly expressed in the old Commentary they are thus stated:

The fiery lives burn within the bosom of Mother.
The fiery centre extends to the periphery of the circle and dissipation supervenes and pralayic peace.
The Son returns to the bosom of Father, and Mother rests quiescent.

A Statement by Apollonius of Tyana

I have studied in my long and numerous travels the wisdom of all countries. Every philosophical sect has presented itself before me, adorned in all the ornaments which belong to each of them, and I have investigated all with the utmost dignity of my being, in order to make a choice. All have allowed themselves diversely pretty, and with a super-human exterior; several have insinuated themselves into my reason with seductive charms, and striven to captivate me by marvelous promises. One has announced to me, lulled in her dreams, that I would be melted with the multitude of her pleasures. Another although boasting not that she would save me from the punishments of life, yet she would show me those ordeals terminated by a sweet and perpetual quietude. This one offers me equilibrium of Soul between good and evil, that one encourages me to venture all, in order to render my future happy. All attach themselves to my hold upon the earth by that which they call legitimate satisfaction of the half of my being.

Only one of these Sages, that of Egypt, has stood aloof, silent and veiled. At last she presented herself, when she found that her companions had not taken me captive. "Young man," she said to me, "I am the daughter of the past and the mother of the future. I am the queen of the spirits and the reflection of God upon the worlds. In order to be admitted into my empire, it is necessary to renounce the vanities of the earth, the sensual delicacies and luxuries of life. I prohibit passional love amongst my disciples as a dangerous folly of the Soul. I commend them to be silent, in order that they may feel themselves always in the presence of God. I abominate blood sacrifice, which supposes that the supreme Being is endowed with the ferocity of a tyrant. I teach filial prayers, which are, with the offering of incense, the only cult appropriate to the Father of all things. If thou hast the courage to follow to the solitary summits, where Truth dwells, I will make of thee a new man . I will give thee new eyes which will open themselves upon an infinite world of Immortal Essences. Thou wilt embrace at one glance all time. Thou wilt comprehend all beings, their secrets. And the Forces of Nature will obey thee." Thus spoke to me the Wisdom of Egypt, the Grand Magian of the Sons of God. I have followed her instructions, and she has faithfully kept her promise to me.

Bibliography

Abhinavagupta. *Paratrisikvivarana*. Translated by Jaideva Singh, 1988.
The Tantraloka.

A Brahmin. *Some Thoughts on the Gita*, 1893. Extensively quoted by Alice Bailey in *A Treatise on Cosmic Fire*.

Adams, W. Marsham. *The House of the Hidden Places*. 1895.
The Book of the Master: The Light Born of the Virgin Mother. 1898. These two highly esoteric works pertain to the greater Egyptian Mysteries.

Aiyar, K. Narayanaswami (translator). *The Thirty-Two Vidyas*. Madras 1916
Thirty Minor Upanisads. Madras 1914 Contains several works of the great yogi-seer Gorakhnath.

Allen, Paul. *A Christian Rosenkreutz Anthology*, 1968. Contains translations of many important and original Rosicrucian works.

Anonymous. *Crata Repoa, Initiation in the Ancient Mysteries of the Priests of Egypt*. 1795. (Reprinted in Manly Hall's *Freemasonry of the Ancient Egyptians*, 1937)

Anonymous. *On Mankind, Their Origin and Destiny*. London 1872

Anonymous. *The Dream of Ravan*, 1895

Attwood, Mary. *A Suggestive inquiry into the Hermetic Mystery*. 1850 (Also contains the complete *Golden Treatise* of Hermes)

Avalon, Arthur. *Serpent Power*. 1918.

Babbitt, Edwin D. *The Principles of Light and Color*. London 1878 (unabridged). This scientific masterwork is still ahead of its time. It pertains to the author's clairvoyant experiments with etheric matter. The editor of the highly abridged edition (less than half of the original), which is now available in bookstores, has removed all that he considered unscientific, which happened to be the best and greater part of the book.

Bacon, Roger. *The Mirror of Alchemy*. L.A. 1975

Bailey, Alice A. *A Treatise on Cosmic Fire.* N.Y. 1925. . The books listed here were written by Master Djwhal Khul and published under the name of his student Alice Bailey.

A Treatise on White Magic,

A Treatise on the Seven Rays. 5 volume set. Volume 5 of this set, *The Rays and the Initiations* and the above *Treatise on Cosmic Fire* was written primarily for initiates. (More by this author)

Bailey, Foster. *The Spirit of Masonry,* Kent 1957. Most of this book was written by Master D.K.

Banerjea, Akshaya. *The Philosophy of Gorakhnath.* Contains a lengthy synopsis of Gorakhnath's *Goraksha-Vacana-Sangraha.* Gorakhnath was a genuine seer. His work, therefore, contains a wealth of little know information on the etheric body.

Blavatsky, H.P. *Isis Unveiled,*

The Secret Doctrine. Adyar Edition, 6 vols. 1938 Contains as the fifth chapter writings of H.P.B. found in papers left behind after here passing along with the here secret instructions to the students of the Esoteric Section.

The Esoteric Writings of Blavatsky, 1907

The Voice of Silence. This book is intended for initiates who are preparing to enter the Greater Mysteries.

Boehme, Jacob. *The Works of Jacob Behmen.* 4 vols. London 1764-1781.

Brunes, Tons. *Secrets of Ancient Geometry,* 2 volume set.

Charpentier, Louis. *The Mysteries of Chartres Cathedral.* Translated by Ronald Fraser, 1972.

Collins, Mabel. *Light on the Path, 1885.*

Through the Gates of Gold, 1887.

When the Sun Moves Northward. These three books were written for initiates preparing to enter the Greater Mysteries.

Corbin, Henry. *Creative Imagination in the Sufism of Ibn 'arabi.* Princeton Univ. Press.

Avicenna and the Visionary Recital. Princeton.

Spiritual Body and Celestial Earth. Princeton.

Costa, Hippolyto Joseph. *The Dionysian Artificers*. Preface by Manly Hall, 1936

Curtiss, Harriette. *Key to the Universe*. 1917

   Key of Destiny 1925 These two very profound masterworks cover the esoteric significance of the numbers 1-22.

   Voice of Isis.

   Message of Aquaria. (More by this author.)

Dionysius of Areopagite.

   Mystical Theology and the Celestial Hierarchies, translated by the editors of Shrine of Wisdom, 1965

   Divine Names, Shrine of Wisdom, 1957.

   Complete Works, Translated by Colm Luibheid, 1987 The works by this author directly or indirectly reflect the esoteric teaching of St. Paul and the school he started in Athens. The writings of Dionysius form the basis for Esoteric Christianity.

Enoch.

   Ethiopic Apocalypse of Enoch, translated by E. Isacc.

   Slavonic Apocalypse of Enoch, translated by F. Anderson.

   Hebrew Apocalypse of Enoch, translated by P. Alexander. These three books are included in the *Old Testament Pseudepigrapha*, 1983.

   The Book of Enoch, translated by Richard Laurence, 1883.

Ferrier, J. Todd.

   Exekiel: A Cosmic Drama. 1931

   Lief's Mysteries Unveiled.

   The Divine Renaissance, 2 volumes.

Ficino, Marsilio. *On Dionysius the Areopagite*, 2 vol. set. Translated by Michael Allen, 2015. Being a commentary on *Mystical theology, Divine Names*

Fulcanelli.

   Le Mystre des Cathedrales, translated as *Fulcanelli: Master Alchemist* by Mary Sworder, 1971

   Dwellings of the Philosophers, 1999.

Gargyayana.

   The Pranava-Vada, The Science of the Sacred Word, 3 volume set. Edited by Bhagavan Das, Adyar 1911.

Gorakhnath.

    The Gheranda Samhita, translated by James Mallinson, 2004

    Goraksha Vacana Sangraha, a synopsis translation by Akshaya Banerjea is his *Philosophy of Gorakhnath.*

Gyatso, Khedrup. *Ornament of stainless Light: An Exposition of the Kalacakra Tantra. 2004*

Guthrie, Kenneth. *The Pythagorean Sourcebook and Library.* 1987.

Hayyan, Jabir ibn (Geber).

    The Works of Geber. N.Y. 1928

Hermes. *"Aureus:" The Golden Tractate.* Profound yet highly veiled.

    The Divine Pymander. Translated by Shrine of Wisdom, 1923

Heindel, Max. *The Rosicrucian Cosmo-Conception.* 1909

    The Vital Body.

    Freemasonry and Catholicism, 1919

Iamblichus. *On the Mysteries and Life of Pythagoras.* Translated by Thomas Taylor. Prometheus Trust.

    On the Mysteries. Translated by Emma Clarke and others, 2003.

Iamblichos. *Theurgia or The Egyptian Mysteries.* Translated by Alexander Wilder. 1915

Ibn 'Arabi, Muhyiddin. *The Universal Tree.*

    Contemplation of the Holy Mysteries.

    Four Pillars of Spiritual Transformation.

    Divine Governance.

    (Other works by this author)

Incagnito, Magus. *The Secret Doctrine of the Rosicrucians.*

Kaplan, Aryeh (Translator). *Sefer Yetzirah: The Book of Creation.* 1997 (Revised ed.)

Kaushik, Dr. R. P. *Organic Alchemy*

Kingsford, Anna. *The Perfect Way,* 1881.

Lakshmanjoo, Swami (Translator). *Shiva Sutras.* 2002

Maitreya. *Heart Essence of the Great Perfection: Three Teachings of Maitreya,* 2016

Matt, Daniel. (Editor) *The Zohar* (Pritzker Edition), 12 vols. As of this printing 8 vols. have been printed.

McDaniel, G. Ivan. *Lamp of the Soul.* 1942.

Mead, G.R.S. *Thrice Greatest Hermes,* 3 vols. 1906 Contains his translations of several masterworks including those of Hermes.

    (Translator) *Pistis Sophia,* 1909

    (Editor) *Five Years of Theosophy,* 1885

Myer, Isaac. *The Philosophical Writings of Solomon ben Ibn Gebirol,* 1888. One of the best of the writings on the Qabbalah.

Paracelsus. *The Hermetic and Alchemical Writings of Paracelsus,* 1894. 2 vols.

Patanjali. *Yoga Philosophy of Patanjali* by Swami Hariharananda Aranya, 1903. Contains his translation and commentary of the *Yoga Aphorisms.*

    Light of the Soul, Being the *Yoga Sutras* translated by D. K. with a commentary by his student Alice Bailey.

Plato. *Works of Plato,* 5 vols. Translated by Thomas Taylor, 1804. Recently published by Prometheus Trust.

Plotinus. *The Six Enneads,* translated by Stephen MacKenna and B.S. Page.

    Collected Writings of Plotinus, translated by Thomas Taylor, Recently published by Prometheus Trust.

Pullen-Burry, Dr. H.B. *Qabalism, 1925*

Proclus. *Commentary on the Timaeus of Plato,* Translated by Thomas Taylor, 1820. 2 vols. Prometheus Trust.

Pryse, James. *The Magical Message According to Ioannes,* N.Y. Theosophical Pub. 1909.

    The Apocalypse Unsealed, 1910

    The Adorers of Dionysos, 1925

    A New Presentation of the Prometheus Bound of Aischylos. 1925

Pupils of E. G. *The Mysteries of the Qabalah, Vol. II, 1922*

Ramacharaka. *14 Lessons of Yoga Philosophy and Oriental Occultism*

    Advanced Course in Yoga Philosophy and Oriental Occultism, 1904

    Raja Yoga, 1906

    The Philosophies and Religions of India. (More by this author)

Rijckenborgh, Jan Van. *The Gnostic Mysteries of Pistis Sophia.*

    The Alchemical Wedding of Christian Rosycross, 2 vloume set.

Roerich, Helena. *Agni Yoga,* 1929

    Hierarchy, 1932

    Infinity, 2 vols. 1930

Fiery World, 3 vols. 1934 (More by this author)

Rosenkreutz, Christian. *The Chymical Wedding, 1690.*

    The Fame and Confession of the Fraternity of the Rosie Cross, 1652

Row, Subba. *Esoteric Writings, 1895*

    Lectures on the Study of the Bhagavat Gita, 1897

Russell, Walter. *The Secret of Light.* 1947

Skinner, J. Ralston. *The Key to the Hebrew-Egyptian Mystery.* 1875

Snodgrass, Adrian. *The Symbolism of the Stupa,* 1985. Undoubtedly the best book on Sacred Geometry available.

Steiner, Rudolf. *The Book of Revelation, 18 Lectures.* 1924

    Mystery Knowledge, Mystery Centres. 1923.

    Initiation, Eternity and the Passing Moment. 1912

    The Temple Legend. 20 lectures on the secrets of Freemasonry, 1904 & 1906.

    Alchemy.

    The Gospel of St. John, 1908.

    The Gospel of St. John 1909. (More by this author)

Straiton, E. Valentia. *The Celestial Ship of the North,* 2 volume set. N.Y. 1927. Later published by Lucis Trust 1932.

St. Germain. (17th century) *The Most Holy Trinosophia of the Comte de St. Germain.* With an introduction and commentary by Manly P, Hall, 1963

St. John. *Apocalypse of St. John.*

    Gospel of John.

Swami Sabhapaty. *Vedantic Raj Yoga.* Lahore 1880

Taittiriya Sanhita. 2 vols. The Veda of the Black Yajus School. Translated by Arthur Keith. Delhi 1967.

Theosophus, Hinricus. *The Secret Symbols of the Rosicrucians,* 1785

    The Golden Treatise on the Philosopher's Stone. (Included in Paul Allen's *A Christian Rosenkreutz Anthology)*

Trismosin, Solomon. *Splendor Solis.*

Three Initiates (Ramacharaka). *The Kyballion, A Study of Hermetic Philosophy.* 1912

Uniche. *The Mysteries of Isis,* translated from the original mythic symbols, *1858*

Valentinus, Basilius. *The Triumphal Chariot of Antimony.* London 1893

Vaughn, Thomas. *The Works of Thomas Vaughan.* Edited by Authur Waite, 1919

Van Rijckenborgh. *The Alchemical Wedding of Christian Rosycross* (2 volumes) Netherlands 1992.
   Egyptian Arch-Gnosis (Corpus Hermeticum) 4 volumes. Netherlands 1982

Von Welling, Georg. *Opus Mago-Cabbalisticum et Theosophicum.* Translated by Joseph McVeigh in 2006.

Waite, Arthur (Editor). *The Hermetic Museum,* 2 vols. 1893

Wallace, Vesna. *The Kalacakra Tantra: The Chapter on Sadhana. 2010*
   The Kalacakra Tantra: The Chapter on the Individual. 2004

Whilhelm, Richard, translator. *The Secret of the Golden Flower,* 1935

Yogananda, Paramhansa. *Selfrealization Fellowship Lesions.*

Zohar: Bereshith - Genesis. Translated by Nurho de Manhar, San Diego 1971

www.ingramcontent.com/pod-product-compliance
Lightning Source LLC
Chambersburg PA
CBHW070707130626
46553CB00005B/1885